C000212945

THE LIFE AND TIMES
OF THE
GREAT EASTERN RAILWAY
1839–1922

The new terminus of the Great Eastern Railway at Liverpool Street, opened in February 1874, replaced the smaller Bishopsgate station and gave the growing commuter traffic from the eastern suburbs better access to the City and to connections for other London districts Illustrated London News, 24 July 1875

The Life and Times
of the
Great Eastern Railway
1839–1922

Harry Paar and Adrian Gray

Castlemead
PUBLICATIONS
WELWYN GARDEN CITY

First Published in 1991

This book is copyright under the Berne Convention. All rights are reserved. Apart from any fair dealing for the purpose of private study, research, criticism or review, as permitted under the Copyright, Designs and Patents Act, 1988, no part of this publication may be reproduced, stored in a retrieval system, or transmitted, in any form or by any means, electronic, electrical, chemical, mechanical, optical, photocopying, recording or otherwise, without the prior permission of the copyright owner. Enquiries should be addressed to the publishers:

CASTLEMEAD PUBLICATIONS
12 Little Mundells
Welwyn Garden City
Herts. AL7 1EW

Proprietors
WARD'S PUBLISHING SERVICES

ISBN 0 948555 26 2

© Harry Paar and Adrian Gray 1991

British Library Cataloguing in Publication Data

Paar, Harry
  Life and times of the Great Eastern Railway.
  1. Eastern England. Railway services : Great Eastern
  Railway, history
  I. Title II. Gray, Adrian
  385.09426

  ISBN 0–948555–26–2

Phototypeset in 10pt Palatino Roman Type by Intype, London
Printed and bound in Great Britain
by The Bath Press, Avon

Foreword

The most abiding image of the Great Eastern must surely be the contrast between the country branches at the extremities of the system, and the suburban network approaching London. In essence, this is a contrast that has survived across the years: although commuters now come to London from much further afield, it is still possible to travel under a wide-open East Anglian sky to a gas-lit station that serves only a pub and a windmill. It is also still possible to sample some of the atmosphere of the old Great Eastern as one travels in modern electric trains from Bishop's Stortford to Cambridge, through immaculate and charming rural stations which retain old GER fittings such as fireplaces.

The Great Eastern Railway had a distinctive charm of its own, but it struggled to match the glamour of bigger companies like the North Eastern Railway, which could boast cathedral-like stations and towering bridges. It lacked the patrician loftiness of the Great Western or the crimson splendour of the Midland. Despite running through a relatively flat part of Britain, it was never a race-track; for a season a Norwich train was the fastest in the country, but grander companies soon recovered their pre-eminence.

The spirit of the Great Eastern lived on long after the Company itself had gone, and Liverpool Street was typical of this. My memories of it in the early 1970s were of a very rambling, complicated and grubby station from which the last steam engine seemed to have departed only five minutes previously rather than a decade before. An indicator board straddled platforms 8 and 9 with information about each train presented using an ill-matched set of boards, all with different lettering styles and shapes. One can only admire those who conceived the transformation of Liverpool Street into a showpiece station for the 1990s. Time alone will tell if there will still be quiet corners where the spirit of the Great Eastern will linger a while longer.

Because the longest journey on purely GER metals was only ever about 130 miles, the Company could never invest in high-speed, multitracked routes, though for a while it acquired a reputation for stately elegance due to its Cromer expresses. No other main line in the country still suffers as tortuous an exit from London as the Cambridge route. It is perhaps because of this that the GER always had to suffer detractors; indeed the criticisms have been very consistent over the years.

Despite all this, the GER came to make a very strong contribution to the prosperity of East Anglia while retaining a character all of its own. Railways still have a unique role to play in East Anglia today, a factor which has been reflected in the creation of BR's Anglia Region.

The GER had a more turbulent history than most railway companies, but was always full of charm and personality. Therefore I hope that this book will not only be enjoyed, but will also widen the knowledge of this most interesting Railway Company.

CHARLES DEVEREUX
BR Route Manager, West Anglia
Spring 1990

Acknowledgements

The authors are grateful to the staff of the following institutions for their assistance:

Bishopsgate Institute Reference Library
Cambridgeshire Collection
Cambridge University Library
Colchester Local Studies Library
Essex Record Office

Guildhall Library, London
Norwich Library Local Studies Collection
Public Record Office, Kew
Redbridge Central Library Local History Room.

The authors are also grateful to their fellow members of the Railway and Canal Historical Society who have provided assistance and advice.

Contents

The Eastern Counties Railway Ballad

The following ballad appeared soon after the opening of the first part of the Eastern Counties line. It may have had two origins: on the one hand it could have been written to celebrate the opening of the railway, on the other it could equally well be a fine example of Victorian satire – especially as the ECR had such a dreadful reputation in its early years!

The line – the line – the Eastern Line!
The firm – the safe – the works so fine,
Without a jolt, without a bound
We're wafted through the scenes around,
With the wind we play – we mock each steed,
While like the lightning's bolt we speed!

I'm on the line – I'm on the line
I am where comforts so combine
With the dome above, and the Lounge below,
And attendants whereso e'er we go:
If a storm comes o'er and rains earth steep,
No matter – I ride on and sleep!

I love – O! how I love to ride
By the power of Watt's fierce, hissing tide!
Where each man's goal is reached so soon,
And whistles sound their warning tune,
To tell that cometh the station near
And why the course must now be clear.

I never pass the old highway o'er,
But I love the railway more and more.
And back I fly to some timely train
Like our Braithwaite when his aid we gain,
And a glory to me it is indeed,
For I so joy on the line to speed!

The hopes were few, and pockets closed,
At the time our line was first proposed.
The scheme was doubted, but men grew bold
When the Thorndon Lord so sought its gold!
And never were such ills to lurk
As at first, against Braithwaite's work.

I have tried, since our first opening day,
Full many a buggy, coach and 'shay',
With time to judge and power to range
But never again shall sigh for change;
And now when I as trav'ller shine
I go by our famous Eastern Line.

Reference here to Braithwaite means the early engineer of railways who was much involved with the ECR and its locomotives in the first days. The 'Thorndon Lord' was Lord Petre whose demand for high compensation delayed construction work.

Artist's view of the Eastern Counties line running across the Lea Valley, 1837. It was produced before the railway opened, and the artist omitted to give the engines a driver or fireman!

Essex Record Office

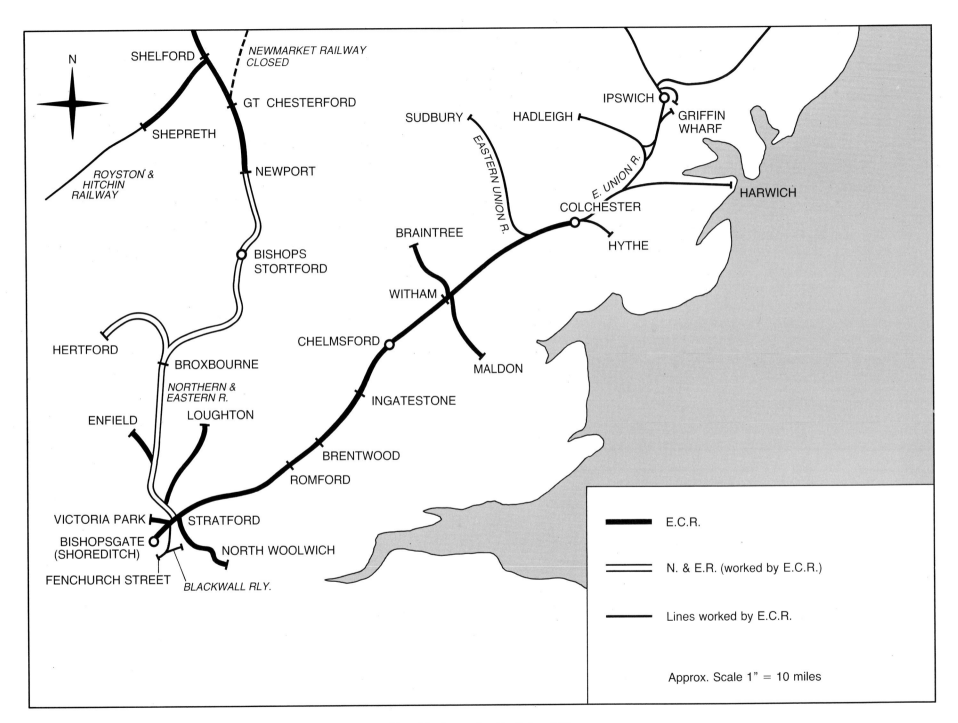

Map of the Eastern Counties Railway 1862

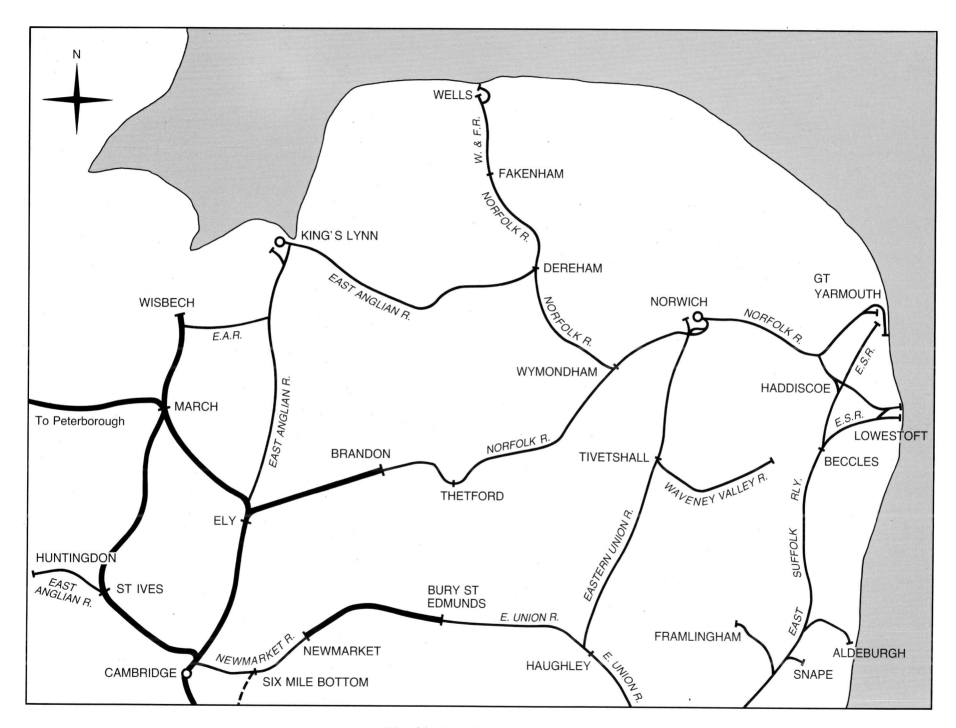

Map of the Eastern Counties Railway 1862

Figure 1.1   *The original ECR station at Norwich Thorpe*
Illustrated London News, 2 August 1845

From Infamy to Efficiency

East Anglia achieved a period of considerable wealth and prosperity during medieval times, when the wool trade helped to make it one of the richest and most densely populated regions of England. Norwich was one of the greatest cities in the kingdom, while the people of East Anglia celebrated their wealth by constructing magnificent churches in towns like Hadleigh and Lavenham. However, the region went into a long period of decline, and finally the Napoleonic Wars hit the last remnants of the wool trade very hard indeed.

When industrialisation began, the region found itself lacking crucial mineral resources such as coal and iron ore, and so was hardly a great attraction to the promoters of the first railways. However all this looked set to change in the 1830s with the first schemes for East Anglian railways. Most of these were rather fanciful and were based on exaggerated claims as to the region's traffic potential. An 1834 scheme, originally known as the 'Grand Eastern Counties Railway', was condemned in the letters columns of the *Essex Standard* as being both 'wild and visionary' and also a 'poor, sickly bantling.'

The first major railways for the region were authorised by Parliament in 1836, only six years after the opening of the Liverpool & Manchester Railway. These projects were the Eastern Counties Railway, to run from London to Colchester, Ipswich, and Norwich with an extension to Yarmouth, and the Northern & Eastern Railway which aimed to build a line from London to Cambridge, with the intention of going on to Norwich and Yarmouth. The first sections to be opened were the ECR's line from Mile End to Romford in 1839, onto which the N&ER joined at Stratford when it opened its line from Broxbourne in 1840. Thereafter, chronic financial deficiency troubled both concerns.

It would be exciting to record a titanic struggle between the two Companies to reach Norwich first, but the truth was quite the opposite. The ECR ground to a halt at Colchester in 1843; in covering 51.75 miles it had spent nearly double the estimated £1.6m for the entire 126 miles to Yarmouth. This included a number of significant problems in purchasing land, plus a costly setback when the bridge being built across the River Blackwater at Kelvedon collapsed due to poor workmanship by the contractors. Meanwhile it took the N&ER much barrel-scraping to reach Bishop's Stortford in 1842 – a mere 29 miles.

The men of influence in Norwich, Yarmouth, and Ipswich were becoming disillusioned and proceeded to promote their own railways to fill the yawning gaps between their towns and the nearest railhead. The first line to be completed was the Yarmouth & Norwich Railway in 1844, which soon amalgamated with a line from Norwich to Brandon to form the Norfolk Railway. On a wider scale, success was at last achieved when through communication was opened between London and Norwich via Cambridge in 1845.

The people of Ipswich could not allow themselves to be forgotten. Under the guidance of John Chevallier Cobbold, a shrewd solicitor, the Eastern Union Railway was formed; it opened a link between Ipswich and Colchester in 1846. Less than six months later, on Christmas Eve, an extension to Bury St Edmunds was opened by a separate company which then amalgamated with the EUR in 1847. The enlarged concern pressed on with a line from Haughley to Norwich which was opened in 1849. Thus the foundations of the East Anglian railway system were laid by a motley collection of minor companies, many of whom were uneasy bedfellows.

The route to Norwich via Cambridge became mainly an ECR affair since that company gained control of the N&ER and also the Norfolk Railway. The alternative route via Ipswich was 12

Figure 1.2 *The opening of the EUR line from Colchester to Ipswich in 1846. Proportion is not the artist's strong point, for the position of Colchester seems mountainous! The impressive building in the centre is the Station Hotel, which was not a success. Fortunately for the EUR, no company money was involved*

miles shorter, but a large part of it was controlled by the EUR and so the Eastern Counties pursued a policy of sending as much traffic as possible via Cambridge. Doubtless the ECR reckoned that it could starve the EUR of traffic and then buy it at a knock-down rate. Such was the harsh reality of railway politics.

The ECR itself was short of money and rapidly became a target for cynical press comment, spurred on by an unfortunate run of accidents. It was accused of having dangerous locomotives, slow and unpunctual trains, and poor carriages. Rumours that its bridges were unsafe were encouraged by local press editors keen to find some controversy, though allegations that the ECR was slow were at least founded in truth: *Tuck's Improved Railway Timetables* of 1849 gave the average speed of

ECR expresses at 26 mph, compared to 40 mph on the Great Western. Local newspapers in Colchester and Cambridge hinted darkly at problems with the track and gave the ECR a number of unkind nicknames, of which the least unpleasant was probably 'the Cinderella of Railways'.

Now at least Cinderella met Prince Charming, but the poor ECR fell into an altogether less honourable embrace in 1845 when George Hudson was invited to take control by a group of worried shareholders. This was at the height of the 'Railway Mania', when railway promotion and speculation reached such a fever pitch that its effects in the City of London were likened to that of the Plague. Unfortunately Hudson, called in to repair the frail economic state of the Eastern Counties, brought dubious financial methods with him: he raised vast amounts of capital for fanciful schemes, paid inflated dividends of up to 8% out of capital, falsified accounts and misappropriated funds.

The storms that began to gather about the ECR were numerous and varied; a suspicious Board of Trade, defective engines and rolling stock, financial blizzards – none of these left the staff untouched. Some railway men suffered physically, some fatally, as we shall recount; others suffered an early and harsh form of redundancy, such as the crossing keepers who were dismissed to cut costs.

Under these circumstances the railway press scented an easy prey and enjoyed a field day when the ECR got into trouble for failure to pay the Poor Rates in an Essex parish. The *Railway Times* for 13 November 1847 reported the incident gleefully:

SEIZURE OF A RAILWAY CARRIAGE FOR POOR'S RATES.
– On Wednesday se'nnight a novel scene took place on the Chelmsford (Essex) station, on the Eastern Counties Railway – nothing less than the officers of justice marching upon the line, warrant in hand, and clutching, with the strong arm of the law, a first-class carriage, in payment of the sum of £31 for poor's rates due to the parish of Margaretting. It seems that the Directors imagined themselves aggrieved by the assessment of the overseers, and gave notice of appeal at the last quarter sessions, when it was thought the question was in a fair train for a decision; but they suddenly stopped short and abandoned the appeal. Still the cash was not forthcoming, therefore nothing was left but to resort to legal compulsion. However, as the trains made no stoppage at Margaretting, but went whizzing, and snorting, and whistling on, as much as to say 'we wish you may get it!' and as cuttings and embankments, and trains and bridges, are not very saleable commodities, it was found necessary to put the law in motion in the neighbouring parish of Chelmsford. Accordingly, a warrant having been issued by a resident magistrate, the carriage, once laid hold of, was committed to the safe custody of strong locks; but we have not been informed whether it has yet been released from the house of bondage to the freedom of the rail.

As his great railway empire began to totter and crumble, George Hudson resigned in disgrace in February 1849. He left behind an ECR that was at best a shambles, at worst a positive

danger to life and limb. A letter to *The Times* in March 1851 summarised the anti-ECR viewpoint and provides an early example of newspapers delighting in anti-Railway vitriol:

[The ECR is] . . . a living embodiment of folly, fraud, delusion, recklessness and suffering; its name is identified with chicanery, mismanagement and confusion, as having passed all reason in the audacity of its construction, and killed Her Majesty's lieges by scores in the first year of its operation . . . reckless disregard of the Sabbath . . . its present total indifference to the comfort, convenience or moral welfare of the poor as regards the third class trains . . .

THE RAILWAY JUGGERNAUT OF 1845

Figure 1.3 Punch's *view of the Railway Mania, with the foolish hordes throwing themselves in front of the train*

This letter, a masterly concoction of exaggeration and half-truth, summarises the Press view of the ECR at the time but also, in its criticism of the ECR for Sabbath-breaking, hints at Victorian middle-class hypocrisy – it was acceptable to make your servants work on a Sunday, but not acceptable for trains to be run on the Sabbath. But with this sort of criticism the ECR began to enter the folklore of the day as a kind of music-hall joke. Thus the great novelist Thackeray is reported to have said: 'Everything comes to an end – even a journey on the Eastern Counties Railway.'

But the departure of Hudson brought no relief from the ECR's misery. Edward Betts, later to achieve notoriety through his involvement in the financially imaginative Peto & Betts contracting partnership, kept the Chairman's seat warm until November 1850 when he was succeeded by Joseph Glynn, who in turn was replaced in March 1851 by David Waddington.

Waddington was known to be an acolyte of Hudson's and had been elected MP for Maldon in 1847, an event surrounding which there is a persistent legend: the allegation is that Maldon owed its fine station building to Waddington's desire to win more votes, either through impressing the locals or by keeping some of his men in town to finish off the work until they had cast their votes. A Parliamentary investigation into bribery and corruption found evidence that Waddington's workers were not really workers at all, but merely voters. A witness was asked of them, 'They did not know what to do with themselves, I suppose?', to which the witness replied, 'No – my old game cock would scratch up more earth in a day than ten of them did.'

In the period 1854–5 the poor Eastern Counties was once more hit by stories of mismanagement. In particular there were reports of continual frauds in the Stores Department; there was

the illegal sale of 2,352 lb of horsehair, and then a man was transported for a fraud involving copper. In January 1855 a strong faction of shareholders managed to blame the laxity of affairs onto Waddington, but a man named Challis stood up to defend him. Subsequent events were reported by a railway press journalist who clearly did not share Challis's views:

> The man went on dribbling, and the meeting went on hooting and shouting, until it had nearly come to blows, a dozen men were speaking and gesticulating at a time.

Figure 1.4 The first station at Elsenham. This was at Fuller's End crossing about ¾ mile south of the present station. Local tradition is believed to be correct in saying that the small locomotives had difficulty in starting northbound trains from a stand due to the adverse gradient, and the station was later moved. The station-house shown survived until 1973   Illustrated London News, 2 August 1845

Waddington was unceremoniously booted out in 1856, to be replaced by Walters and then Horatio Love. Love was a member of the London Stock Exchange and had been involved in trapping the errant George Hudson in February 1849. Love eventually retired to Margate, where his Director's Pass was found in the sand by a little girl in 1900.

By the time Waddington had left, a number of other problems had emerged, many of these connected with an engineer, Peter Schuyler Bruff. Bruff had helped Joseph Locke on the construction of the Eastern Union Railway in 1844–6 and afterwards built several other lines throughout East Anglia. In 1854, when the working of the EUR was taken over by the ECR, he became engineer to the combined system – a case, perhaps, of a man accepting the poisoned chalice!

In August 1854, while the ECR was still controlled by Waddington, the Permanent Way Inspector had reported that 'The whole of the Ways and Works are in a satisfactory and efficient state of repair.' This Permanent Way Inspector was Peter Ashcroft, who in March 1854 had been acquitted of manslaughter at Norwich after a very strange accident in snow near Thetford. He then secured a job with the South Eastern Railway, where he became involved in further controversy, leaving Bruff to handle a situation that was far from 'satisfactory'.

The track and bridges of the ECR had been reported to be in an appalling state. When these rumours reached Norwich Corporation, the Board of Trade was called in to investigate the apparent dangers to its citizens. It must be said that it was largely a fear of accidents which motivated the Corporation, rather than actual events, for the ECR had improved its accident rate since 1852. Colonel Wynne inspected the line for the Board of Trade and his report, dated 26 February 1855, referred to defective ballast, rotten sleepers and decaying bridges. The timbers of the viaduct over Sir William Beauchamp's Navigation, for example, were said to be so bad that 'in many parts these timbers could be dug out with a spade like garden mould.'

Waddington, still in control, retorted 'I cannot assent to the conclusion that it is dangerous to traffic.' Bruff, however, was given the job of repairing the line without interrupting traffic, estimating that £100,000 was needed for repairs and a further £50,000 for improvements. The ECR also set up a Permanent Way & Works Committee, which began meeting in October 1855.

Bruff made a full report to this Committee, dated 25 October 1855. He complained that 'The renewing of your perishable works has been delayed too long by years' and he catalogued the problems that needed attention. There were difficulties with 'many hundreds of timber bridges spread throughout your whole system' whilst 'many large and hazardous structures are fast verging to destruction.' Bruff referred to 'the gravity of the position in which I have been placed since my appointment.' His priorities were the unsafe bridges, the permanent way ('the removal of rotten sleepers and worn rails etc do not involve such fearful dangers'), while stations were the least pressing concern as they involved little risk to personal safety.

The main problems were on the Norwich via Cambridge route and also on the Ely to Peterborough branch. Bruff was directed to repair the bridges without too much disruption to traffic. Thus special orders had to be issued such as those of 14 January 1856 which instructed that 'safety travelling inspectors' should ride on every engine between Broxbourne and Norwich to ensure the correct observation of speed limits on the defective bridges. Each bridge was to be protected with special green boards indicating the speed limit; a diamond meant 15 mph and a triangle 10 mph – difficult to judge in an age when engines lacked speedometers. If the inspector suspected that the train was going too fast, he was advised to time the number of seconds taken to pass between seven telegraph poles and report the matter to the Outdoor Superintendent at Bishopsgate.

Colonel Wynne inspected the progress that had been made under Bruff on 31 December 1855, but was rather hesitant in giving the line a clean bill of health. The *Cambridge Chronicle* deplored this view and also lambasted *The Times*, which was filling up a quiet period of the year with a spot of ECR-bashing:

The Government Inspector and *The Times* between them make it appear that every man who travels upon the line escapes mutilation only by a miracle; no doubt their frightful statements have had bad effect upon several old ladies of both sexes.

The Permanent Way Committee resolved that, in view of the problems with the wooden bridges in the Fenland district and on the Cambridge line, the officers should divert as much traffic via Ipswich as possible. On 10 January 1857 Bruff was still so disenchanted with conditions on the ECR that he wrote in a critical vein to *Herapath's Railway Journal*. The ECR Board were not pleased, but Bruff argued that 'questionable circumstances' justified his action. Bruff perhaps saw further trouble and even

disaster ahead and was trying to protect himself. The *Cambridge Chronicle* of 21 February 1857 carried an advertisement from Bruff to the effect that he was relinquishing his post as ECR engineer and explained the situation he had inherited when he first took the job – 'the whole country was in a state of alarm; persons refused to travel on account of the dilapidated and dangerous condition of the works . . . '

One of Bruff's last acts was to tell the Board that the bridges between Peterborough and Whittlesea were so poor as to necessitate a 2 mph speed limit. Then he left the ECR, but this was not the end of Bruff's contribution to East Anglian railway history. He had been elected to membership of the Institute of Civil Engineers in 1856 and now built up a career as a free-lance engineer. Amongst other achievements, he was responsible for

Figure 1.5   Punch's *view of an ECR Board Meeting. The early time is part of the satire!*

Having made another Wrong Move, how many ——**Caps** *will you require?*

the Waveney Valley Railway and the Bury & Thetford; he was also involved in a property scandal over the Tendring Hundred Railway.

John Viret Gooch, the locomotive superintendent, was another who saw 'something nasty in the woodshed' when he joined the ECR in 1850. Finding, as one source primly puts it, 'much need for reform and improvements', he set to work with a will. However, when cosy, inefficient practices are disturbed by a new broom, much dust is likely to fly – and so it was with Gooch. Some of the enginemen went on strike and replacement drivers were so hard to find that three locomotives were damaged by inexperienced drivers before new men could be brought in, mostly from Scotland.

According to Cusack Roney, who was Secretary of the ECR at the time of the strike, there was also some deliberate damage to engines, though mostly of a minor character. The ECR sacked many of the strikers and sent a list of 'the names of engine and firemen who recently combined to compel the directors to discharge their Superintendent' to many Railway Companies, including the EUR which still worked its own trains at the time. The aim was to have the offending men blacklisted for a year, and Roney later claimed that they came back to him in desperation:

> The more necessitous of the men appealed to the author, and to his brother officers, to be reinstated. Many a man . . . accompanied his appeals by tears . . . by degrees, as vacancies occurred, some . . . came back into the service. But they came back at the bottom of the list of drivers . . .

Gooch survived and kept his job until Waddington ran into trouble. A report criticising Waddington's Chairmanship was issued by some shareholders on 27 December 1855. This was followed by a poll as to whether Waddington should be returned to the Chair, which he won sensationally by 712 votes to 683. This result was then overturned when it was found that 552 of Waddington's votes were proxies. Gooch was one who had feathered his own nest during the period of Waddington's

mismanagement, earning a comfortable £600 per year plus a percentage of what was saved by fuel economy. In addition he had a profitable sideline as a partner in a coal firm which prospered due to an advantageous trading relationship with the ECR. Interestingly, this firm collapsed when Gooch sold his interest! With the demise of Waddington, Gooch saw that his own days were numbered and left in 1856; as an 1860 pamphlet put it, he retired from the ECR 'as a well-bred dog walks down-stairs when he sees preparations on foot for kicking him out of the window.'

1860 saw a campaign to restore Waddington's reputation through the publication of a notorious Blue Book compiled by an anonymous group of shareholders, but the equally anonymous author of *A Few Facts and Figures* condemned it with typical Victorian invective:

> I will not be a party to the administration of a poisonous nostrum, under the pretence that it is a wholesome stomachic. The quack's tincture of rhubarb is laudanum, and his bitter aloes strychnine. The dose is poison.

Perhaps one of the problems of the ECR was that it had grown, by the late 1850s, from a company that operated a short line running out as far as Romford to one that operated most of the railways in East Anglia, yet it had not developed an effective regional management structure. Thus the officers at Bishopsgate dealt with a large number of matters, both trivial and important, many of which would have been better handled by men on the spot.

For example, when the Traffic, Locomotive & Permanent Way Committee met on 6 July 1859 the Chairman of the Company, Horatio Love, introduced what he presumably regarded as an important matter – and it was solemnly resolved that a dust bin be erected at Maldon station. The Committee then went on to spend its valuable time on an even more prestigious issue, a consideration of the number of rats killed at various stations between 3 and 30 June. Thetford topped the poll with 37, but

Kennett was apparently in the heartland of rat-hunting country, for no less than 150 met their Waterloo 'in the immediate vicinity of Kennett station.'

Such issues show that men like Love continued the pre-industrial style of management – a detailed, personal interest in all that went on, rarely delegating responsibility to promising employees. However, it is also likely that with the rapid expansion of the nation's railways there were simply not enough capable, trustworthy men to staff the outlying districts; certainly the early stationmasters included a number of men who fell short of the standards for which their profession later became noted. On 19 May 1857, for example, Mr Bale, holder of the august post of stationmaster at Bishopsgate, acquired a house at Brentwood and moved his furniture down the line in two vans and a horse-box – without getting permission first. The Traffic Committee decided to tell him that 'it is incompatible with the responsibilities of a station master for him to reside at any place out of the immediate vicinity of the station and that he cannot be allowed to reside at Brentwood . . . he has acted very wrong in the transmitting of his furniture . . . ' As a final, ominous, note, Bale was told that the Chairman would 'see him'.

Whatever was known, or not known, about railway management, the ECR Board certainly understood the importance of management perks in image creation, especially when it came to the 'management toilet'. Soon after the Bale episode, the committee noted that the directors had been put to 'inconvenience . . . by the occasional use by the clerks of the private washing room' at Bishopsgate, and they resolved that 'the room on the second floor of the south side of the station (lately occupied by Inspector Chaplin) be fitted up as a washing room for the clerks.' To each his appointed place!

Having gained a reputation for wasting money on a cata-

strophic scale in its early days, the ECR then changed to a policy of saving money at all costs. As we have seen above, this sometimes led to bad publicity. In January 1861 there were severe snow storms in Norfolk and some Norwich people set up a 'Committee for the Relief of the Poor'. The Mayor wrote to the ECR about the urgent need for cheap coal in the City; prices were so high that the poor would freeze to death. The ECR Secretary wrote back in a distinctly frosty manner, promising only to 'lay the matter before the Board' at their next convenience. This was not the sort of urgency that the people of Norwich required and local newspapers slammed the ECR once more: 'Rapid motion, even on such an occasion, is too costly for the ECR', one wrote.

Pinxton Colliery agreed to send 200 tons of coal at 15s 6d a ton to Peterborough. The ECR responded sluggishly to this and it was not until March that the Chairman reacted to press criticism by ordering best efforts to be made in delivering the coal. The Norwich Committee felt that it would have cost the ECR little to make a charitable reduction in its freight rates.

However, not everything about the ECR was bad. It was early to experiment with patent signals (1843), it was the first to use wheel rim weights for counter-balancing (*c*.1844), it conducted early experiments in burning coal rather than costly coke (1845), it was almost certainly the first railway to introduce light locomotives (1847), and it constructed the first compound locomotive in 1850. By the 1850s it had recovered enough to be running some fast expresses, averaging 48 mph, which was exceeded only by the Great Western and Great Northern. Speeds of 70 mph were recorded in 1856.

Other companies built railways in East Anglia and joined the ECR in various ways. Notable were the East Anglian Railways serving King's Lynn, Ely, and Huntingdon, and the Newmarket Railway which achieved fame by being one of the first railways to close a substantial line. By mid 1854 all the major railways of Essex, Suffolk, and Norfolk were effectively controlled by the ECR, but it was not until 1862 that their fusion was completed with the formation of the Great Eastern Railway. This

Figure 1.6   (On facing page) Colchester North Station in the early 1870s. Note the former hotel, converted into an asylum some 20 years before. Goods facilities are fairly limited, though the brick field has its own siding   Ordnance Survey

ANOTHER WRONG MOVE

BY THE

NOTORIOUS EASTERN COUNTIES RAILWAY BOARD.

"The **Board**" is in a *dreadful stew*
  On EASTERN COUNTIES RAIL,
And clearly don't know what to do
  About the "**Donkey tale.**"

It seems enraged, and thus to cry—
  "Ye noisy, grumbling men,
We will not thus be taunted by
  Your jeering, caustic pen.

"You Tottenham men are very rude,
  And saucy as a monkey ;
We know your views are low and crude,
  Though you cry out for "**Donkey.**"

" Although the Public voice is strong,
  You shall not laugh at us,
But if you fancy we are wrong,
  Why go, and take '*the Bus.*'

" Ye little men that deal in Fish,
  May think it very funny,
But plain we say, we do not wish
  To touch your dirty money.

" Ye trading men who go to Town
  To buy your sundry wares,
Remember this—though you may frown,
  We'll charge you **higher Fares.**

" For while you to the third class creep,
  To save a little cash,
You'll see that we are quite as deep,
  For we will spoil your '*Hash.*'

" **Day-Tickets** from our Line, for thirds,
  We'll stop this very day,
And those whose anger quickly curds,
  Our **single fares** shall pay.

" The man who can't afford our Fares,
  On *marrow-bones* may go ;
We care but little what *he* cares—
  Our "CONSEQUENCE" we'll show.

"And those who to the markets rush
  On every market day,
We'll quickly from our Railroad brush,
  Or make them *richly pay.*

" We'll teach you all, both high and low,
  Where'er our trains may run,
That though our "**Donkey Line**" *is slow,*
  We'll not be *quickly* done.

" The **TRAINS** *were slow*—they're *slower now*:
  We'll "Lord it" from this station :—
The **FARES** *were high*—they're *higher now*—
  The Highest in the nation."

Figure 1.7 One of a number of 1850s ballads ridiculing the ECR. According to the ballads, Hoy's donkey-cart had outpaced an ECR train over many miles
Herts Record Office

comprised the Eastern Counties, Eastern Union, the East Anglian, Norfolk, and Newmarket Companies.

The new GER had advantages and disadvantages. On one hand it had a well-defined territory to serve with an adequate but not excessive network of lines. It was almost free from rivals except at its north-west and southern sides. But on the other hand it had no manufacturing or mineral base to create traffic and it served a rural area with few large towns. Also, there was the awesome legacy of the ECR – it was hardly possible to recover within a decade from a nightmare like the management of the line by Hudson and Waddington.

So the GER continued to have problems and on 2 July 1867 was placed in receivership. For a time a few of its locomotives carried humiliating metal plates saying that they were the property of various creditors. The GER lost a Bill in Parliament to raise £1.5m additional capital but, as the railway historian Acworth wrote, 'The Company amended their Bill, asked for £3m, and got it.'

The GER's financial recovery was partly the work of Samuel Laing, who had joined the Board in February 1867, but it was never a particularly prosperous company. Instead, it gradually developed a reputation for efficiency under a succession of able Chairmen – Lord Cranborne, later Marquess of Salisbury (1868–71), Lightly Simpson (1871–4), C. H. Parkes (1874–93), and Lord Claud Hamilton who, after many years as Deputy Chairman, succeeded Parkes in 1893. Major improvements were made during this era, such as the construction of the GN & GE Joint Line connecting the GER to Doncaster and the coalfields. The superseding of the small Bishopsgate terminus by Liverpool Street laid the foundation for a spectacular development of commuter traffic, but at considerable cost, while the GER also became renowned for its fast expresses to Cromer. Continental traffic was encouraged by a new port at Parkeston Quay (named after Parkes) opened in 1882. By 1914 the GER had progressed

Figure 1.8 *Norwich Thorpe Station at the time of its rebuilding in 1886*

Norwich Library

a great deal from the sickly ECR which Professor Jack Simmons has described, simply, as 'inept'.

In concluding this brief introduction, we may observe that railways were products of individual ingenuity, intended to meet the needs of communities of individuals in their material hopes. Thus, perhaps inevitably, they were always less than perfect, sometimes tragic, not infrequently comic, and always interesting – and rarely more so than in the eastern counties. It is hoped that these very human aspects will be demonstrated in the following chapters.

2

Accidents and Incidents

RAILWAY AMALGAMATION—A PLEASANT
STATE OF THINGS

Passenger. "What's the matter, guard?"
Guard (with presence of mind). "Oh, nothing particular, sir. We've only run into an excursion train!"
Passenger. "But, good gracious! there's a train just behind us, isn't there?"
Guard. "Yes, sir! But a boy has gone down the line with a signal; and it's very likely they'll see it!"

2.1 A Catalogue of Disasters

It was often said that the companies which formed the GER had an alarmingly high accident rate, and this was reckoned to be especially the case with the ECR. This reputation was at least partly due to a number of well-publicised accidents in the early days. This was made worse by early rumours of reckless driving, hardly necessary since the ECR's schedules were among the slackest in the country.

The six earliest locomotives were 2–2–0s with six-foot driving wheels. Of these, No. 3 was derailed between Bow and Stratford on 21 June 1839; another early accident near Brentwood on 19 August 1840 was blamed on the reckless driving of the 7 pm train from Brentwood on the down grades near Putwell's Gate. The engine involved was 2–2–0 No. 6. Initial reports said that the train came off the track due to excessive speed, killing four people including driver Foster and fireman Ebsworth. However, attention soon focused on the instability of four-wheel passenger engines, and the Board of Trade enquiry showed that the use of four-wheel engines with large wheels was unusual. It was suggested that extra wheels should be placed beneath the firebox on these 2–2–0s, but there were also complaints that the line from Romford to Brentwood had been opened before it was safe for traffic. Then on 14 September 1840 No. 5 collided with the train in front when running light to Stratford; a passenger was killed.

A few weeks later another up train from Brentwood came to grief, this time 1½ miles short of Stratford. The tender and a second-class carriage became derailed as a result of faulty

Figure 2.1 *An early railway cartoon gently illustrates public concern over safety, probably inspired by the bad record of the ECR* Punch

wheels on the tender. The guard had the worst fright – he was seated on the roof of the derailed carriage and had to cling on with all his might. His position was not an unusual form of exhibitionism, but the normal practice of the day.

More serious was an accident near Bow in late 1840. This was on a busy section of line, since ECR trains out of Shoreditch shared tracks with N&ER trains going to Broxbourne. This section of line between Shoreditch and Stratford was governed by several regulations, including a time interval of ten minutes between departures from Shoreditch. In foggy weather trains were not allowed to stop at wayside stations like Bow and Mile End. From 8 October 1840 the time interval had been extended by five minutes, but this failed to prevent the accident near Bow station that winter. The ECR's 10 am down slow train left 4½ minutes late on a foggy morning, with a load of five carriages. It passed Devonshire Street station but then made an unauthorised stop at Bow.

Meanwhile, the following N&ER train, driven by Edward Hindley, had pulled out of Shoreditch at 10.14½ am – five minutes sooner than it should have done. The Inspector at Shoreditch had used hand signals to try to stop Hindley's departure, but to no avail. Due to the weather Hindley should have limited his speed to 15 mph, but he passed Bow station in 4½ minutes, indicating a speed of 45 mph according to one source. Just beyond Bow the N&ER train ran into the back of the ECR one, smashing the rear carriage and causing several injuries.

The N&ER, which was extending its line from Bishop's Stortford to Newport, was leased and worked from 1 January 1844 by the ECR, which secured powers for a line from Newport to Cambridge and Brandon. There, it joined the line being built by the Norfolk Railway from Norwich. The whole line from Stortford to Norwich (Trowse) was opened to the public on 30 July 1845, and within a week a serious accident occurred on the ECR section. On 4 August the 11.30 am down train, hauled by a Norfolk Railway locomotive, was derailed near Littlebury tunnel, north of Audley End. The fireman and the guard were killed; the latter had also been on the carriage roof and was killed when he lost his balance. Local journalists flocked to the scene, intent on a first opportunity to exercise their tortuous prose, as in the *Cambridge Chronicle*:

> The engine and tender were lying on the bank belching forth torrents of steam and smoke, and almost surrounded by red-hot coke; and already were the luggage van and horsebox in flames, from their close contiguity to the fire: the carriages were thrown about in various directions upon the line, all of them more or less injured, some with wheels off and others stove-in in several places.

General Pasley inspected the scene of the accident, and the local press reported him as saying 'I should not be afraid to go at 50 mph on a line like this.' None the less, Pasley blamed the accident on excessive speed and suggested that gradient posts should be put up to warn drivers of downhill sections. This was long before speedometers were heard of. At the time many felt that poor construction of the railway may also have contributed to derailments. Just before the opening of the line north of Cambridge, an embankment subsided beneath a works train, indicating likely dangers in the future. Just after the line opened, a train was derailed at Waterbeach on 19 August 1845. It would seem that heavy rains had made the works unstable, and no steep gradient could be blamed in the middle of the Fens!

On Christmas Eve 1845 an up Norwich express came to grief between Harling Road and Thetford, driver Pickering and fireman Hedger being killed when it went over the embankment. The engine went down one side of the line and the carriages down the other. Pasley again blamed excessive speed but was also suspicious about the construction of the engine; this was one of the 'White Horse of Kent' type 2–2–2s, a Robert Stephenson product.

Another extraordinary accident which can be blamed on human error occurred on the Newmarket Railway on 12 May 1848. The 3.30 pm train from Newmarket stopped at Dullingham, where the engine was detached to do some shunting. The brakes on the passenger carriages were not applied properly, and the trainload of passengers were astonished to find themselves gradually rolling backwards! It was three miles downhill to Newmarket, with much of the line steeply graded at 1 in 109, so the runaway train picked up considerable speed. The *Railway Times* described the end of its journey, saying that 'it dashed with great force into the Newmarket terminus, from which it had started, to the no small consternation of the passengers, who were most of them thrown violently from their seats.' There were four serious injuries, but the results could have been much worse had another train been on the line.

Following the report in the *Railway Times*, the Secretary of the ECR wrote in to say that his Company had nothing to do with the management of the Newmarket Railway, an understandable precaution in view of the ECR's bad name for accidents.

Nearly 20 years later, in 1867, the Harwich branch train was left at Manningtree without properly applied brakes and then rolled backwards, fortunately giving a passing main-line train only a glancing blow.

When railway staff were at fault in an accident they were often arrested and could be tried for manslaughter if there was a fatality. An example of this was the trial of a stoker following the death of driver Wilson at Ingatestone in 1851. The two

Figure 2.2   *The 2.55 pm up boat train was derailed near Bradfield, Essex, in July 1864, the stoker being killed. This sketch, by a passenger, gives a rather exaggerated view of the gauge of the track*   Illustrated London News, 23 July 1864

men were responsible for an up Colchester luggage train. At Ingatestone they stopped to shunt back into a siding for the passenger train to pass, but a coal wagon derailed and blocked the points. The driver got out to investigate but the stoker started the engine and crushed poor Wilson between the coal wagon and some carriages. The *Essex Standard* reported the scene vividly:

> So firmly was the poor fellow fixed that nearly twenty minutes elapsed before his body could be extricated, when life was found to be extinct, and from the nature of the injuries sustained it is thought death was instantaneous.

Wilson's wife was ill at home and it was reported that, when the news of her husband's demise reached her, she died also. The stoker was tried for manslaughter but found 'Not Guilty'.

'Learning the road' was a vital part of a driver's training, but it was not always done thoroughly. In October 1854 a goods train from Sudbury was approaching Marks Tey in the care of a driver new to the line. He should have halted for the points to be set but instead continued and ran into a siding, colliding with the loading dock. The engine and four trucks were knocked over, but at least simple safety precautions had prevented the train running onto the main line at the junction.

Minor accidents like this were a common problem, but were still considered worthy of a paragraph in the local newspaper. If there were injuries, then an accident had news value further afield. In February 1874 a GER Fenchurch Street to North Woolwich passenger train collided with a Midland Railway goods on a crossover near Stratford. At least ten people were injured. Initial reports blamed the GER driver for ignoring signals but it was soon proved that the train's brakes had failed to stop it on the descent to the crossover.

Faults with an engine caused two fatalities at Stretham near Cambridge in 1882. The driver of the 5.15 pm from Cambridge was travelling at over 45 mph when he saw an object fall from an engine approaching on the other track. The object proved to be a 3 cwt 'balance weight', and the driver of the 5.15 pm

Figure 2.3   *An unfortunate accident on Lavenham Bank, 16 October 1895*
Suffolk Record Office

had no chance of stopping. Engine and tender struck the weight and were derailed, rolling over into the dyke beside the line; a number of passengers were injured. Mr S. Cushing of Walthamstow suffered compound fractures of the legs; he refused to have an amputation and tetanus set in causing his death. The other fatality was an old lady who was waiting to meet her daughter and grandson off the 5.15 pm; she became very excited at the news of the accident, and when they finally arrived safely she had a stroke and died.

Accidents to goods trains occasionally revealed interesting

details about freight traffic. A 'continental' goods was derailed near Colchester in June 1867 after the couplings snapped. Three or four of the 25 trucks rolled down a high embankment, spilling imported ducks, groceries, and wine everywhere. It was not reported whether the local people 'salvaged' any of the goods.

This accident compares with the 'Great Continental Egg Smash' near Aldersbrook (Ilford) at Christmas 1899. A derailment resulted in millions of imported eggs blocking three of the four running lines!

Minor errors often resulted in only minor incidents, but tragically they could also cause major disasters. Carelessness caused three injuries at Witham in 1874 when empty carriages for the Maldon line were shunted onto the wrong track. An up Colchester train ran into the tender of the Maldon locomotive and smashed it to pieces. Traffic was stopped for three hours and a queue of seven trains built up at Chelmsford. This accident was, of course, minor compared to the tragic high-speed derailment of a Cromer express in Witham station in 1905, which caused the death of eleven people, making it one of the worst in GER history. This was a result of men working on the track being careless about the approach of a train.

A large number of fatalities occurred through the public getting onto the track, especially in the early years. Not all understood the necessary precautions: the inhabitants of Coggeshall in Essex, legendary for their slow-wittedness, were said to believe that the fences along the lineside were intended to stop the trains getting out and attacking ordinary passers-by! A sad example of incidents resulting from people getting onto the track was at Whittlesford, south of Cambridge, in January 1847. Two young women went to the station to watch their sister depart for London. They crossed over the line to the up platform since there was no footbridge, but had a lengthy wait since the London train was late.

The girls saw their sister off to London and, as the last carriage rolled by, stepped out from behind it to cross back over the line. The stationmaster shouted a desperate warning that a down express was coming, but to no avail. Fortunately a porter

had been stationed between the tracks to prevent people crossing, and he was able to drag one of the girls out of the way by pulling her clothes. The other girl was struck by the down express, following which a search for her remains was started. The *Cambridge Chronicle* described what was found:

> The first object that attracted attention was a bonnet, and one of the porters lifting it the head of the poor girl fell out. A few yards higher up the line was found the trunk, shockingly mutilated, one of the arms severed, and part of the right leg.

Another incident of this type occurred at Stonea, in the Fens, in April 1854. This time a group of friends were crossing the line with their dog as a train was approaching. The dog was unaware of the danger and, just as it seemed about to be killed, a girl from the group dashed forwards to rescue it. She was herself knocked down, and her friends ran home in terror. Some platelayers rushed to the scene and found that her dog, sitting beside the badly-injured girl, would not let them touch her. Happily she recovered from her injuries.

On 22 August 1859 the driver of the 1.10 pm Cambridge to London via Hitchin train was passing the Shelford Road bridge when he saw a horse and cart move onto the occupation crossing directly in front of his train. The cart was driven by an old woman and had several children as passengers. Driver Wilson had no time to stop his train and so his engine struck and killed the horse, and 'dashed the cart to pieces'. The 75-year-old woman was dragged from her perch on the disintegrating cart and 'carried on the motion bar of the engine' for 60 yards; then the train was stopped and 'she was extricated from her perilous position.' A number of children were bruised but otherwise uninjured. The old woman's miraculous escape was further enhanced by press claims that the children were hers – remarkable, considering her reported age.

On 18 September 1866 an Ely to Cambridge ballast train collided with a horse and cart near Waterbeach. The cart was 'broken to pieces' but the horse and its driver, a lad named

Extraordinary Railway Accident.

Anent our article and illustration dealing with the Cambridge Railway Station in the 'forties, Mr. Samuel Cowles, of 13, Little St. Mary's Lane, has sent us along a copy of the Illustrated Times for 1859 containing the above sketch of "an extraordinary railway accident at Shelford" in August of that year. The publication states: A correspondent has forwarded to us a sketch (which we have engraved this week) and a brief account of a most remarkable accident that occurred a few days since on the Cambridge line. As the passenger-train from Cambridge to Hitchin neared the bridge at the Shelford Junction an old woman drove on to the rails just in front of the engine, which was going at a speed of twenty miles an hour. The horse and cart were literally dashed to pieces, and, although there were four children besides the old woman in the vehicle, strange to say, they all escaped unhurt. The old lady herself was pitched on to the engine across the top of the motion bars, her head resting against the driving-wheel splasher. In this position she was carried a distance of seventy yards before the driver could manage to pull up. Save for the fright and some slight disarrangement of her attire, the old dame seemed none the worse for experiences of an unusual system of railway travelling.

Figure 2.4   *The accident of August 1859 at Shelford*   GER Magazine

William Camps, escaped injury. He was, however, 'injured' by the magistrates, who charged him with costs of 18s 6d.

Suicide also became a problem. In January 1894 the headless body of a man was found on the line near Markshall, between Norwich and Ipswich. The head was found 20 yards away. The dead man proved to be George Hawes, a labourer from Lakenham who had last been seen the previous evening. An inquest was held in a nearby shepherd's hut, a tiny building that measured only 14 ft by 10 ft. It was concluded that Hawes had deliberately placed his head on the line and that he had probably been run over by the 6.5 pm from Norwich Victoria.

In another grim case, David Bartrop's mutilated remains were found on the GER at Leyton on 10 February 1894. A verdict of 'Wilful Murder' was recorded, but the murderer was unknown.

A month later the 'victim' of an accident was the GER swing-bridge at Somerleyton, which was hit by the steam-wherry *Topaz*. The wherry was following its normal practice of passing under the bridge, but the captain had forgotten that it was high tide and that the wherry was 'light'. The *Topaz* hit one of the bridge girders, and the Somerleyton stationmaster rushed to the scene. The 9.27 am Lowestoft to Yarmouth ballast train was allowed to cross, but subsequent passenger trains were diverted via Beccles.

Derailments occurred frequently; some were of little importance, but others – like Witham – were very serious. Probably the most embarrassing derailment occurred on 1 March 1866 when the first public train into the new station of St Botolph's in Colchester came off the track and delayed the station's opening. The train had come from Weeley and had just left Hythe when the locomotive and its tender came off the track at the junction. The engine was running tender first, with a train of two carriages and a brake van. Twenty passengers were thus prevented from being the 'first' into St Botolph's, with the opening being delayed until the next day when a train actually made it to the terminus.

A fractured left-hand tyre on the 2–2–2 No. 103 hauling the 7 am up Cambridge train caused a derailment at Tottenham on 20 February 1860. It took place while the train was travelling at 35–40 mph, with serious results. Locomotive Superintendent

Sinclair watched in horror from the station as the engine struck the platform and turned over, with the tender flying over it. 'Enginer, tender, and some of the carriages were heaped upon each other; while piteous groans emanated from the mass of ruins, and the steam from the engine enveloped everything in a dense mist', a journalist reported.

Fireman Barber was 'smashed to pieces' and Driver Rowell, who had to be dug out of the wreck, was scalded to death. Fireman Cornwell was also killed. The two other fatalities were Mr Satchell, a hatter, and Mr Stokes from Saffron Walden. Enquiries showed that the tyre was faulty at the weld, but the ECR Locomotive Department was unable to supply a history of the tyre. Captain Tyler said that the Department needed urgent reorganisation; Sinclair said he was trying to sort it out – but he had already been in the post for 3½ years. After the accident the ECR received a letter from W. Freeland of Saffron Walden and Charles Shepheard of Moorgate Street, City, requiring the Company to preserve the broken tyre, wheels, and locomotive in case they needed to be examined for the legal process.

Another fractured tyre caused the 5.17 pm Clacton and Walton train to Colchester to come to grief in February 1890. 0-4-4T No. 137 was hauling 17 vehicles and was within 500 yards of Wivenhoe when a tyre broke as it rounded a curve. The enginer rolled over and went down the embankment, whilst the brake van was smashed by the following carriage. For the train's guard this was the third accident in 18 months – he had had lucky escapes at Thorpe and Colchester North. There were two serious injuries.

At least the ECR and GER suffered no major catastrophes through the forces of nature. High winds, flooding, or snow caused occasional problems, but deaths were usually the result of human folly. Thus the Thetford disaster of 1854 occurred in snow but was caused by human error, and the Thorpe collision owed little to the appalling weather that night (for both incidents see below).

Flooding was responsible for the construction of the Mildenhall branch. Severe flooding near Lakenheath in 1878 encour-

aged the GER to build the branch with the ultimate intention of carrying it through to Thetford as a complete alternative to the Lakenheath section. In 1880 the general manager told the Board, 'We have suffered and shall suffer again from floods stopping traffic on the main line at Lakenheath. The local parties have repaired the former damage with silt only and it will give way again . . . Altogether the flooding has cost the company £40,000.' The line was built to Mildenhall, but proper repairs to the flood-prone section proved effective, and the new branch progressed no further.

In the Fens, flooding could cause trouble. For example, in 1862 the Watlington to Wisbech line was closed for a while after the collapse of the Middle Sluice caused widespread flooding. The worst flooding to strike the GER occurred after the torrential rain of 26 August 1912. It was calculated that 1,000 million tons of rainwater fell on Norfolk alone. Inland lakes developed, including one two miles wide between Tivetshall and Beccles, while the Fens reverted to their natural state! Norwich lost all its rail links for 2½ days after eight inches of rain in one day.

The worst damage was on the Norwich main line between Flordon and Forncett, with initial diversions being made via Brundall, Reepham, and Ipswich. Then this line itself became flooded at Cantley, although hasty repairs at Lakenham allowed the Forncett to Wymondham line to be used instead. Porters from Harwich Parkeston Quay were taken to Melton to help move passengers around a breach in the line.

Part of the platforms at Homersfield were washed away. The Cantley to Brundall section was closed for several weeks and the Fakenham to Wells line until 10 September. The worst problem was the three-span bridge on the main line between Forncett and Flordon, which had been undermined at its middle pier by floodwaters and had collapsed at 5.10 pm on 26 August. A repair gang arrived at 1.30 pm on 27 August and on 1 October two 'Claud Hamilton' locomotives were used to test the new structure; traffic recommenced the next day. A tablet was fixed on a pier of the bridge to record the flood level.

Snow caused the odd problem too, like the collision between

a luggage train (several hours late) and a 'Parliamentary' train at Colchester in 1861. Heavy snow obscured the driver's vision, so it is fortunate there were no serious injuries. (All railways were required, by an Act of 1844, to run at least one train daily along every line at a minimum speed of 12 mph and a maximum fare of one penny per mile.)

The GER was one of the few railways in Britain ever to have its services disrupted by an earthquake. The Colchester quake occurred on 22 April 1884 at 9.20 am, with its epicentre about five miles south of the town. Mr Blatch, the Colchester North stationmaster, was ready to flag out the 9.20 am to London when he heard a rumbling sound. He felt the platform heave under him and he fell back to the wall. He saw an engine and some coaches rise and fall, jostling one another it seemed, whilst windows cracked and doors flew open. The driver was thrown out onto the platform and the passengers, some bruised and cut, scrambled out as quickly as they could. There were no more trains out of Colchester that day, as engines had to be sent out to test all the bridges.

At Ipswich, Mr Nibloe the stationmaster also felt the shock and heard noise. At Chelmsford the signalman in the elevated box was so scared by the swaying of his building that he believed its collapse was imminent. He was thrown against the levers, and other observers commented on the strange jerking movement produced in the signals by the quake.

At Witham the signalmen saw their indicators moving erratically and felt the boxes sway. Men at work in the coal yard saw the coal heaps moving and feared that the water tank would topple over.

Many sightseers travelled to Colchester the following weekend, arriving in crowded trains from north and south. On the Sunday a special train had to be run. It seems, however, that the epicentre being several miles away from any railway saved the GER from a major disaster.

2.2 Explosions

One of the most common accidents on the early railways was the explosion of locomotive boilers. A typical occurrence was that at Maldon in February 1852, remarkable in that no one was injured.

The locomotive that erupted in such spectacular fashion had, according to the *Essex Standard*, been transferred to the ECR from the London & North Western Railway. However it may in fact have been ex-Midland Railway 2–4–0 No. 71, bought by the ECR in 1847 and sold on to the Colne Valley Railway in 1860. At its moment of fame it was being used for menial duties on the Maldon branch. On the fateful morning it had prepared for the 8 am departure from Maldon and was waiting at the platform while the driver and fireman followed the regulation of giving their names to the guard.

It was this attention to duty that saved them, for while they were off the footplate their locomotive was destroyed in an explosion. Thomas Turner, Maldon's senior porter, was standing next to the first carriage and was showered with glass from the 'passenger arcade' or roof. The blast severely damaged the station, depositing a piece of iron from its roof in the telegraph wires. A rail beneath the locomotive was pushed into the ground with great force, shattering the sleepers.

Damage, at over £2000, was considerable, but no one was injured. A fault in the engine was suspected, but there was little solid evidence for Mr Gooch to study when he began his investigation.

On 17 April 1859 the down Ipswich mail train met disaster near Ilford. The train had just passed the station when the locomotive exploded in such a spectacular fashion that the sound was heard in Barking. Miraculously, both driver and fireman survived, though they were thrown yards onto the lineside bank. The driver received head injuries, the fireman was unharmed.

2–4–0 locomotive No. 74 was not so lucky. Its boiler of 'common iron' with longitudinal plates had burst, with the driving wheels ripped off, leaving only the firebox and smoke-box behind on the line. Other parts of it were scattered for yards in every direction. Several carriages were derailed, but there were no injuries amongst the passengers. Sinclair told the Traffic Committee that 150 of their engines had boilers of the same type, and he had had one bound with wrought iron bands as an experiment. This was the same engine as that involved in the disaster at Thetford, discussed below.

Some explosions, however, were more deliberate. The sound of exploding fog signals used to be common on the railways, especially around London which was for long notorious for its thick, yellow, and lethal fogs. Fog signals detonated by gate-keepers, signalmen, or policemen alerted train drivers to adverse signals in fog, and the guard could also protect the rear of his train in the event of a breakdown. Snow signals were also developed, these being very similar but fixed to the track by driving nails into the sleepers, and the spent cases had to be removed afterwards. If they were not fixed the 'snow brooms' (snow-ploughs) would sweep them off.

The exploding fog signal had not always been standard practice on the ECR. In 1840 the Company sent some sample blue flares to the Liverpool & Manchester Railway for trial use; however, in 1844 the L&MR adopted Cowper's fog signal as recommended by the Board of Trade and this became standard throughout Britain.

The ECR 'Signals & Regulations' book of December 1846 included five pages of 'Directions for the Use of Cowper's Signals in Foggy Weather or in Cases of Danger or Great Emergency'.

No number of regulations could safeguard against slovenly employees, and an accident involving unscheduled explosions was inevitable. In June 1851 a child was killed by the explosion of a fog signal at Manea, between March and Ely. As was usual in such accidents, human folly was involved. A crossing keeper found an unusual type of fog signal on the track; a train had run over it but it had not exploded. The keeper picked it up and showed it to two platelayers, who tried to explode it by striking it with a hammer. Eventually they succeeded, and shattered metal from the explosion struck one of the platelayer's children in the neck. The two-year-old died in five minutes.

The ECR set up its own fog signal factory at Stratford. This exploded in 1857, killing a Mr Beckwith who had been 'in the constant habit of passing the fog signal factory at Stratford in the course of business with the Company.'

This came at a bad time for the ECR, coinciding with the attack on its safety standards by its own engineer, Peter Bruff. Now it was faced with a number of lawsuits for damages, including one on behalf of Beckwith's children. The ECR solicitors were asked to investigate whether or not the case should

Figure 2.5 *Placing a fog signal*   Illustrated London News, 14 December 1844

20

be fought. In August 1857 the solicitors reported to the Board:

> The Company would not, in our opinion, have been liable if there had been no want of proper care and precaution in carrying on the manufacture . . . but . . . it appeared that there were so many circumstances from which a jury would infer negligence and their inclinations would tend towards that conclusion such as the quantity of gunpowder in the place, the employment of boys with iron nails in their shoes, the locality of the buildings, etc. . . . Our counsel was of opinion that there was not the slightest chance of our obtaining a verdict.

The Beckwith family claim was therefore settled for £1,000, and another claim for £250.

Christmas 1848 arrived with a bang for the citizens of Witham, delivered courtesy of the ECR. In fact some were lucky to see Christmas at all, since this was reported to have nearly demolished a section of the town – perhaps an example of a story growing in the telling.

In the very early hours of 23 December a down luggage train arrived at Witham station. The guard told the porters that he had a barrel of gunpowder each for Maldon and Braintree in the last truck. It was a very long train, and the porters had to walk right down the line as far as the Chipping Hill bridge before they got to the last truck.

The barrels were unloaded and then left carelessly on the up track, the porters forgetting about the gunpowder in their haste to deal with an up mail train that was expected at any moment. The down luggage train then pulled away, leaving the gunpowder forlorn on the other line.

Just as the up mail pulled away from Witham station there was a huge explosion, 'driving all the fire out of the firebox of the engine, lifting the engine itself completely off the rails, and tearing up part of the permanent way . . . '

The train disappeared in a dense cloud of smoke, to re-emerge in a shattered state as the cloud dispersed. Driver and fireman were thrown onto the tender but survived, and none of the half dozen passengers were injured. A rail where the engine had been was bent almost double by the blast, and the nearby Albert Hotel lost 46 panes of glass whilst all the beer mugs were blown off the shelves.

What had happened was simple: the gunpowder barrels left between the rails of the up line had been crushed when the engine passed over them, and then the heat of the firebox had ignited the powder.

James Upton was identified as the guilty porter. He was fined £5 by the Magistrates, but they also blamed the ECR for employing insufficient staff. Surprisingly, the town of Witham had some sympathy for the man who had nearly wrecked it and a subscription was started for Upton after it was learnt that he had been sacked. Perhaps he was a lucky man – if the crew of the up train had been killed, he could have faced manslaughter charges.

The only recipient of praise was the Chipping Hill bridge, which survived undamaged. It was alleged to be the 'the best piece of workmanship on the line between London and Colchester'; given the reputed standards of the ECR, this was rather faint praise.

At Bishopsgate station space beneath the arches was rented out to various tradesmen for stables, stores, and workshops. One of these tenants was a coachmaker named Lewis, who practised his craft beneath the Woolwich platform. On 4 June 1857 he was attempting to cook stew for his dinner when he mistakenly poured turpentine into it instead of water. This casued a 'conflagration' and panic in the station above. It caused consternation among the Directors when they discovered that there were many inflammable materials stored in the arches of their station and a wooden viaduct even had Mr Goldsmith's stables beneath it.

2.3　Disaster in the Snow: Thetford, 1854

January 1854 was a bleak month in East Anglia, with heavy snow falling throughout Norfolk and Suffolk. Railway traffic was badly disrupted so that a Wednesday afternoon train from

London to Norwich had to be terminated at Ely. The passengers, among whom was E. Ball, MP (a prominent ECR shareholder and a former director of the Newmarket Railway), were forced to spend the night in the Fenland city.

The worst snow had fallen in the Breckland district, disrupting traffic particularly between Thetford and Harling Road where the telegraph was out of action. Steps taken by the ECR to reopen the line on the following day were to lead to confusion, chaos, and finally six deaths.

The events of that fateful day were so confusing that initial reports in the *Norwich Mercury* bore little similarity to actual events. The true story would have seemed farcical had it not been so tragic.

On this Thursday afternoon in January, the stationmaster at Thetford had become concerned about snow on the track between Thetford and Harling; he was also worried about the loss of telegraphic communication. His solution was to send Guard Briggs on a loco to Harling, with the instruction to form a short train from there back to Thetford, using the down line. Briggs was told to stop any train that he might pass on the up line, and to ensure that no train proceeded westwards from Harling until Briggs himself had returned to Thetford. Stationmaster King of Harling was told about this when Briggs reached him, the purpose of the trip apparently being to check that the line was open for traffic. With Thetford station guarding access to the down line, and Briggs passing on the instructions, there should have been no problem.

Some time after Briggs had left Thetford, a down special from Cambridge arrived there. This was being run to rescue the passengers stranded the day before and its passengers included Mr Ball. According to Ball's own account, this train had two locomotives and some 60–70 labourers aboard, the latter being brought along to do any snow clearance work that might be needed. Onto the footplate of this train stepped William Howard, the district permanent way inspector, who had written out the orders sent to Harling with Briggs.

In the belief that Briggs might return from Harling at any

Figure 2.6   *Thetford Station after its opening. Compare the photograph of the station taken some thirty years later, shown in Figure 3.7*
Illustrated London News, 2 August 1845

time on the down line (as he had been told to), the special set off on the up line, which was the wrong one for normal running. It was believed that Briggs would have stopped any up train proceeding beyond Harling. Briggs himself had been told that nothing would leave Thetford until his return there, but clearly would have been astonished to learn that Howard was disobeying his own instructions.

Meanwhile another special – an up train – had arrived at Harling from Norwich. This also had two locomotives but only four carriages. On the train were two senior officers of the ECR – Superintendent Peter Ashcroft and Permanent Way Inspector J. Latham.

At Harling they were stopped by Briggs and King, who explained the plan to them. This was at 3.45 pm, Briggs having been at Harling since 2.20 pm.

Latham, though, decided to overrule King and continue the up journey. It was later to be pointed out that a stationmaster on the ECR had absolute jurisdiction in his own station, but Latham and Ashcroft showed no sign of listening to a subordinate even though the rule book showed them to be in the wrong. Their train steamed out of Harling at 20–25 mph, using the correct up line – the same line on which the special had left Thetford.

At a point near Bridgham the two drivers saw each other's trains and shut off steam in order to avoid a collision. Realising that the situation was hopeless, the drivers leapt for safety, as did William Howard, who was on the footplate. The firemen were not so lucky.

The trains collided head-on at about 4.20 pm. 'The shock was frightful, all four engines being shattered.' Four men were killed almost immediately, including the two firemen, a carpenter and a platelayer; the latter two were in the gang of travelling labourers. Fireman George Baldwin was transfixed by an iron bar from the loco which pierced him, and his foot was reduced to bare bone by the escaping steam from the engine – it took him an hour to die.

The other fireman was found dead beneath the wreckage and two passengers died in their carriages, two others dying later.

Mr Ball was relatively unhurt and rushed to help. A few years later the *Cambridge Chronicle* reported his description of the events:

> He found the men lying bleeding on all sides. Gentlemen in the carriages were so injured that they could do nothing; but he,

being unhurt, exerted himself to the utmost, rescuing the sufferers from the debris.

The injured were taken to Thetford where Ball gave out brandy to them. He listened to the dying words of Reverend Bell, one of the passengers.

Ball was much praised for his role and later told Waddington, the ECR Chairman, that it would be nice if his free pass over the system could be struck as a gold medal as a family memento. This suggestion was later used by Waddington in a bitter struggle for control of the ECR in 1855–6, it being hinted that Ball had tried to use the situation for personal profit.

Back at Bridgham, however, further disaster was only narrowly averted when the down Norwich mail was prevented from running into the wreckage.

Following the Coroner's inquest, indictments for manslaughter were recorded against Ashcroft, who was Superintendent of the Line, and Latham (who was responsible only for Yarmouth to Wymondham). Part of the evidence was that an ECR rule stated the importance of obeying a stationmaster at all times, and the men who had disobeyed this rule were held to be responsible for the disaster.

The two men were tried in Norwich in March 1854 but were quickly found 'Not Guilty'. In a sensational development the Judge called the whole trial 'a pretence' as the two men in the dock were clearly not to blame; he hinted strongly that Howard, who had disobeyed his *own* order, was the guilty man.

The *Norwich Mercury* felt that the Judge's comments were 'erroneous' but none the less further extraordinary scenes followed. Latham and Ashcroft were treated to a celebratory dinner at the Royal Hotel, with one of the guests being the Coroner who recorded the initial 'manslaughter' charge. Clearly this Coroner must have disagreed with the decision of his own court!

The next serious snowfall to afflict the ECR was in January 1861. That year the ECR kept its trains running very well, despite deep snow near Wymondham once more. All trains were run with two engines and, crucially, a greater number of officials were employed to regulate traffic. Schedules were also eased considerably, and no accidents of note occurred. For once lessons had been learnt.

2.4   Night of Despair: Thorpe, 1874

> The most serious collision between trains meeting one another on a single line of rails, if not the most serious railway catastrophe as regards the number of lives lost and serious injuries, that has yet been experienced in this country . . .

These grim words were written by Captain Tyler, the Board of Trade's inspector into the accident that took place in the parish of Thorpe, just outside Norwich, on 10 September 1874. A head-on collision between two passenger trains on a wet and stormy night, it was the blackest moment in the GER's history and an infamous chapter in British railway history. As with many of the worst Victorian disasters, and just like the Thetford accident, it was caused by plain human error.

Although it was 30 years since railways had first reached Norwich, the Norfolk railway system was still evolving in 1874. Thus the line out of Thorpe station was double-track only as far as Thorpe Junction, where the London and Yarmouth routes diverged. Thorpe station itself, which served Norwich rather than the village of Thorpe, had only two main-line platforms. From Thorpe Junction the Yarmouth line headed towards Whitlingham Junction; the line was single track but a second track had been laid down ready for the opening of the East Norfolk Railway which was to diverge at Whitlingham. Beyond Whitlingham the GER had obtained powers to double the line as far as Brundall. Brundall to Reedham was already double-track, and beyond this there ran two single-track routes to Yarmouth and Lowestoft respectively. There was thus a bottleneck between Thorpe Junction and Brundall; this single track was to prove disastrous.

Many single-line railways at this time were already being worked on the 'Train Staff & Ticket' system, which meant that a driver could not proceed onto a single-line section until he had taken possession of the staff or had signed a ticket to acknowledge seeing it. The GER had not introduced this practice on the Thorpe Junction to Brundall section, stating that the running of irregular fish trains (three or four a day) made it impossible.

Instead they operated a telegraph system between a telegraph office on the down platform at Thorpe station, and the stationmaster's office at Brundall. 'Special telegraph books' were kept in which all single-line messages had to be recorded. At Brundall, stationmaster Platford was in charge, though he occasionally allowed his young son to operate the telegraph. A more complex system applied at Thorpe where clerks were meant to send messages given to them by day or night Inspectors; all such messages had to be signed by the duty Inspector before being transmitted.

The system was unwieldy and open to abuse. It also did not cater for the steady increase in traffic over the Yarmouth line – a third up in 15 years. Now, on a stormy night with late-running trains and with habit taking the place of cautious planning, the staff at Thorpe failed to concentrate on their duties.

On 10 September the 5 pm down express from London was, as usual, running late. Its normal schedule allowed for a short 'turn round' at the Thorpe terminus, and then departure for Yarmouth at 9.10 pm. As the rain streamed down over Norwich, however, the clock ticked towards 9.15 without any sign of the train's approach; Cooper, the Inspector who had just started night duty, began to wonder about changing the running arrangements.

His problem was that the late-running 9.10 out of Thorpe often caused delay to the up mail from Yarmouth and Lowestoft, which had to wait at Brundall to get a clear run on the single line. Cooper had a wealth of experience, having been night Inspector for 15 years, and knew the procedures very well: if the express looked like being 25 minutes late he would tell the telegraph clerk to summon forward the up mail from

Figure 2.7   *Extricating the dead and wounded from the Thorpe disaster of 1874*
Illustrated London News

SCENE OF THE COLLISION.

THE "THREE TUNS" INN, THORPE.

CLEARING THE LINE.

Figure 2.8 *Views of the great disaster near Thorpe in September 1874*
Illustrated London News

Brundall. Cooper spoke to Sproule, the Thorpe stationmaster, about the running arrangements and may have interpreted Sproule's vague comment 'We will soon get her off' as being permission to summon the up mail from Brundall when it could also have been a reference to the late-running down train.

At about 9.15, Cooper went to the telegraph office and dictated a message for the clerk, Robson, to send. The message read, 'Line clear for the up mail before the 9.10 down train leaves Norwich.' Cooper did not sign this message so Robson should not have sent it out, but the young man was possibly distracted by having some friends in the telegraph office and at 9.21 sent the unsigned message to Brundall.

Cooper turned away from the telegraph office, his mind perhaps confused by the discussion with Sproule, the Thorpe stationmaster. Sproule wanted to send a 'short' train on to Yarmouth in advance of the 'down' express so as not to keep local passengers waiting; Cooper did not like this idea. At 9.23 both men turned round to see the late-running express leaving the ticket platform outside the station and moving into the shelter of the Thorpe 'covered shed'.

Meanwhile the unauthorised message from Thorpe had been received on the telegraph at Brundall by Platford's 12-year-old son. Platford then gave the mail train permission to proceed and it steamed out of Brundall at 9.28 pm. Platford himself must have been weary, since he had been on duty since 6.30 am.

At Thorpe Robson, the clerk, wasted valuable minutes sitting and chatting to his friends. While he did so Parker, the day Inspector who usually finished work at 9 pm, readied the express for its departure to Yarmouth. It was Parker's habit to remain at work until he had seen off this train, but the presence of both Inspectors on the station only added extra confusion to the procedures; Cooper assured Parker that the mail train had not been summoned forward from Brundall, so the 'down' express was authorised to depart.

Only after the 'down' train had left, at 9.30 or 9.31, did it occur to Robson that a mistake had been made. Six or seven minutes had been wasted in idle chat, but now it was too late. Robson alerted the horrified Cooper that the mail train had already been summoned forward. Frantically, the Inspector ordered another message to be sent to Brundall – 'Stop mail.' Almost immediately the dreaded reply came back from Platford – 'Mail gone.'

There was now nothing the men at Thorpe could do to avert disaster. Even the signalman at Thorpe Junction was powerless, since he had no equipment to tell him if the line was clear or not.

The only chance was that the drivers would spot each other and bring their trains to a standstill. This had happened on the same section of line in 1853, when two trains had been brought to a stop 'almost touching each other'. But that had been in daylight, on a dry and sunny day. Now it was dark, wet, and stormy; there was little chance of the down express stopping on the slippery rails that descended at 1 in 228.

The two trains met head on at a point two chains east of the first bridge over the old course of the River Yare. A hundred yards further west and the wrecked trains would have plunged into the river, adding further horror to the scene.

Passengers had been huddled in the carriages, protecting themselves against the storm raging outside, when suddenly it seemed to explode into the train. Dr Eade felt a heavy blow, then his carriage was split open and he was thrown out into the marsh. Thrown downwards and sideways into pitch darkness, battered by an immense cacophony of sound, it was a moment of terror for the victims. Eade saw 'one engine broken to pieces, and the other engine on its side with the steam escaping in most unpleasant proximity to his ears.' Another eyewitness told the *Norwich Mercury* that 'the roar of the steam as it escaped from the smashed boilers could only be likened to the roar of enraged wild animals intent on each other's destruction.'

On either side of these mortally wounded beasts lay the chaos which was all that remained of two passenger trains. But the first problem for those quickly on the scene was how to make sense of it all:

The darkness of the night and the fury of the elements, for the rain poured down in torrents, loud peals of thunder rolled around, and there were repeated flashes of lightning, added to the awful nature of a calamity whose extent was then unknown.

Men struggled to reach the scene of the crash to lend assistance, including many of the navvies who were in the district for the building of the Cromer line. They found an awesome sight. Carriages of both trains had mounted each other, creating:

> . . . a heap that looked almost like a three-storey house. The top of one carriage was carried on to the telegraph wires, and other portions of the vehicles were crushed to the very smallest fragments. The rear carriage of the down train hung from the

Figure 2.9   The wreck of the Cromer express at Witham, 1 September 1905. Chelmsford photographer Fred Spalding produced a series of postcards of the accident

bridge over the river, and one at least of the passengers was precipitated into the water.

The victims were widely scattered in the darkness, the *Mercury* reporting that 'Dead and dying were lying in heaps; the wounded were groaning; and the rain falling at the time tended to make matters worse.'

Some passengers were found to have had miraculous escapes. Mr R. Wentworth White was cut out of the wreckage after three hours buried under a pile of mail carriages that towered 'at least sixty or seventy feet from the ground.' An unnamed woman had an even more remarkable escape:

> One lady found herself in Mr Herbert Day's garden, almost denuded but unhurt: she must have been thrown through the fence and trees for her clothes to have been so completely torn off.

The mail guard, Ellis, was thrown through the side of his van. Dazed and bleeding badly, he picked himself up, collected together his mail sacks, and walked to Norwich Post Office with them. There the Postmaster tried to get him to go to hospital, but Ellis would only agree to being taken home to Yarmouth in a carriage.

Another gentleman and his wife on the up train had been so annoyed by the behaviour of another passenger that they had changed carriages at Reedham; they were unhurt, but the carriage they had travelled in at first was totally smashed.

Others were not so lucky. The rescuers spotted a man's head in the wreckage but after labouring to raise the debris and free him, they found that it was completely severed. A woman's leg was found hanging in the wreckage and a girl had her leg amputated on the spot.

The bodies were taken to the covered skittles alley at Thorpe Gardens Inn for identification. Those who were killed or died later included the drivers and firemen of both trains and many local tradesmen. Among the dead were a leather-seller, a clothier, a retired church minister, two members of the West Norfolk Militia, a confectioner, a harness-maker, and a surgeon. Passengers continued to die for some time after the accident; Jane Faulkner's death was recorded in the *Norwich Mercury* of 31 October, which stated she was the 26th person to die.

The GER rapidly announced its own explanation of the disaster: 'The cause of the accident was through the night inspector at Norwich giving wrong instructions to Brundall to send on the up mail to Norwich.' Cooper was suspended from work the next day but this was only the start of a series of inquiries.

First came the City Coroner's Court, which reached a verdict of manslaughter against Cooper and Robson. The hearing was marked by strong feelings between the two men; Cooper asserted that he had told Robson not to send the message and claimed that the telegraph clerk's account was a lie. The Board of Trade's inspector, Captain Tyler, complained that the Coroner's investigation should have been held over until he had finished his own study of the events.

The County Coroner's Court then weighed in with a verdict of manslaughter against Robson, but only charged Cooper with carelessness and neglect. This view was strongly condemned by the London press.

Captain Tyler paid much closer attention to the method of working the single line. Within a few weeks the GER was already starting to replace the telegraph with the Staff & Ticket system. Tyler said that it was Cooper's responsibility to ensure that no mistake over messages occurred; Robson had sent the message improperly, had wasted valuable minutes until the express had left, and had probably been distracted by having others in the office. Tyler also felt that the system of working the line was too complicated and allowed mistakes to be made.

Both men were tried at the Lent Assizes in 1875 for manslaughter. Robson was acquitted, but Cooper was found guilty and punished with eight months in prison. This was a light sentence for the times.

The accident was the signal for numerous 'scare stories' to

Figure 2.10   *The Colchester derailment of 12 July 1913. Two heavy cranes clear the debris on the following day*   LCGB K. Nunn Coll.

circulate in the press. One anonymous letter described confusion over the operation of the Staff & Ticket system on the single line between Wymondham and Wells. It was said that two passenger trains had arrived at Fakenham from opposite directions, but could not proceed as no one had seen the staff. They had to await a goods train from Dereham, but that arrived without the staff also! Clearly the train staff had beaten the human staff on this occasion!

3

The Traffic

The passenger services of the GER can be most clearly viewed as being a fortunate development after the early problems of the ECR, but though they were at times even famous they were never, of course, perfect. One of the reasons for this may lie in a criticism of GER management made by Professor Simmons – that its staff and its directors were too often London men, and the country end of the line never got an even representation.

GER services fell into a number of categories but there were three classes of traffic in particular: firstly, the slow and ambling country trains of legend; secondly, the proud and luxurious expresses on the Cromer line; thirdly, the intensive commuter services around London that gave the GER a total for passengers carried that exceeded its nearest rival by 40% at its peak.

E. Foxwell, writing in 1889, commented that the GER had built up a reputation for excellence after 'an unparalleled history of robbery and general misfortune . . . ' Foxwell also believed that the GER had largely created its own traffic by a policy of encouraging suburban and seaside traffic by such tactics as cheap fares and regular services.

The short but important extension of the line from Bishopsgate to Liverpool Street, decided on in 1862, was part of a broad policy to develop suburban traffic that had been held back by the ECR's tendency to run infrequent and expensive trains. Thereafter the GER invested heavily in lines to help this trade grow, such as the line to Chingford. From 1872 Hackney Downs enjoyed an intensive service of six trains an hour while workmen were encouraged to commute by the low fares – 2d from Enfield before 6.30 am, though the fares increased to 5d at stages during the peak. In 1891 Parkes observed that the cheapest workmen's trains could be profitable if they carried 500 passengers each.

With the opening of Liverpool Street for suburban trains on 2 February 1874, considerable opportunities were grasped and daily passengers had reached 200,000 by 1912. The problem of how to handle this traffic was solved by Sir Henry Thornton and F. V. Russell, who introduced the 'Jazz Service' in 1920 – claimed to be the very pinnacle of steam-powered commuter services ever. By 1924 the Jazz Service, inherited by the LNER, had taken Liverpool Street's daily passenger total to 280,000, nearly double the 1985 figure! And at that time there was a peak on Saturdays too!

Perhaps typical of the GER suburban branches was that to Chingford, which was opened to a temporary terminus there in 1873 and then to a permanent station nearer the town in 1878. Chingford and Walthamstow achieved immediate and rapid growth with the improved transport to London. The fares were not so low that the real 'workmen' could use the trains, but a service of half-fare trains attracted 'better-to-do workmen, with a certain admixture of clerks and others' to

Figure 3.1 *Billericay Station in about 1900. Though the station looks imposing, there is little suburban development to be seen. The locomotive seems to be a Holden T19 2–4–0*
Colchester Library

30

Walthamstow. The GER took advantage of the 1883 Cheap Trains Act, which aimed to alleviate the pressures of the urban slums by encouraging the poor to move to the suburbs via a tax rebate to railways that ran 'workmen's trains'; by 1887 the GER was claiming back £27,000 per year for the Walthamstow traffic alone, yet few were really ex-slum dwellers.

In 1899 the legal process caught up with this anomaly and a compromise was arrived at, with 3d tickets being introduced in 1899 – though they were not advertised until 1901! The legal debate revealed that large numbers of 'workers' caught the early trains to save themselves money, then sat around at Liverpool Street for an hour or two eating their sandwiches. Young lady workers were said to be in moral danger from the practice.

Yet the cost of saving money was often hopeless overcrowding. In 1920 Henry Thornton found that a typical down peak train to Chingford carried 1,463 passengers at its most loaded stage, though how he counted them must be a mystery. This would make an average of twenty people per compartment! Many compartments may have carried thirty people. Not even the improvements of the Jazz Service could totally alleviate the misery this implied. Yet all who lived along the line were dependent on it, so misery or not, Chingford station sold 537,409 single or return tickets and 1,049 seasons in 1922.

Just as it set out to develop the commuter traffic, the GER also tried to build up a seaside trade. This was not only about holiday traffic but about commuting too, for the wealthy could be tempted out of London to live beside the sea.

There were few towns on the GER that could claim to be old-established resorts. Towns like Clacton were a generation or three behind Brighton. So the GER had to create its own famous resorts and the town that gained most, perhaps, was Cromer. On 3 November 1895 the GER ran an experimental non-stop train from Liverpool Street, but regular non-stop services had to wait until water troughs were provided at Tivetshall in 1896. In August the GER began a Sunday evening service from Cromer, non-stop Norwich to Liverpool Street, designed to tap the wealthy 'weekend' market. From 1 July 1897 this grew into

Figure 3.2 *Inner London services on the GER in 1914. A Y65 Class No. 1302 on a Canning Town to Victoria Park working*   LCGB K. Nunn Coll.

a summer daily 'Cromer Express', non-stop between Liverpool Street and North Walsham. The service reached its heyday in 1907–14 as the 'Norfolk Coast Express', but it never regained its prestige after the Great War.

Thus the GER services were characterised by crowded, hustling commuter trains and proud, exclusive expresses. And somewhere down the line, on remote Norfolk or Suffolk branches, ambled the country trains with 'no one to pick up and no one to drop.'

3.1 Prize-fight Specials

The reputation of the ECR was so low in mid-Victorian Britain that it would probably have surprised no one to learn that the

Company was actively encouraging illegal activities by running special excursions to prize-fights.

Prize-fighting or pugilism was the ancestor of today's boxing, but in the 1840s it was illegal. None the less large numbers of people were keen supporters of it, even having their own magazine in *Bell's Life*. Fights could not be held in London due to the difficulty of keeping the Police away, so by the 1820s the sporting fraternity had taken to organising regular steamer trips down the Thames to remote pieces of marshland. There, bets could be taken and battle done without the authorities spoiling the sport.

Railways offered a far better way of getting to a remote place especially if the train could be stopped at a point where there was no road access. Even better were places close to the borders of several counties, since the prize-fighters believed they could thwart one county's authorities by stepping across the boundary into another administrative territory.

One of the first fights to take place in our area occurred near Six Mile Bottom, on the border between Cambridgeshire and Suffolk, in October 1840. One of the fighters, Brassey, stayed at the Queen Victoria in Newmarket, whilst the rival Caunt stayed at Littlebury. The vicar of Cheveley planned to interrupt the proceedings with a force of 'specials', but was diverted on a wild goose chase into Suffolk.

The Champion of England in the early 1840s was Benjamin Caunt of Hucknall. After his triumphs in 1841 he went on a tour of America, returning with a seven-foot giant named Charles Freeman. Caunt ran a stage show in which he sparred with Freeman, but eventually the giant was put in the ring for more serious contests.

A fight was set up for 2 December 1842 between Freeman and William Perry, who was also known as the 'Tipton Slasher'. The plan was that those involved in the fight would travel up to Sawbridgeworth, where the village was in Hertfordshire but the station in Essex, on the 9.30 am train on the day of the fight, thus not giving the magistrates advance warning. This plan was spoiled by a large number of poor pugilism fans, who

went up by road the previous night and thus gave the game away.

Sawbridgeworth station was soon besieged with eager fans, so the organisers of the fight decided to get out of the train at Harlow and travel by road further into Essex to Hatfield Heath. Unfortunately the Hertfordshire magistrates followed them across the county boundary and prevented the fight from taking place. Many of the supporters then streamed back to Bishop's Stortford station, but the protagonists met on the canal towpath at Sawbridgeworth, where they fought for 70 rounds over 84 minutes. By then it had become so dark that they had to stop for the night: there was great difficulty in getting back to Sawbridgeworth station and some spectators fell into the canal. Freeman returned to Harlow station.

The following week a re-match was held at Thriplow Heath, near Littlebury. The Slasher travelled up by train to Bishop's Stortford, from where there was a great demand for carriages to the scene of the fight. The proceedings were interrupted by Captain Robinson and some Police, who followed the party across several county boundaries. After this it was too late to fight – but it was also too late for the last train back to London!

By April 1848 the ECR had clearly realised that there was money to be made out of prize-fights. For a fight at New Shardelows, near Fulbourn, 300 people arrived by express train. The fight took place in a field so close to the railway that the defeated boxer was lifted out of the ring and straight into the railway carriage from which his backers had watched the fight.

In June 1850 a championship fight was held at Mildenhall Road (now Shippea Hill) between 'Bendigo' and Paddock, for £2,000 a side. The location was chosen apparently as being equally convenient for Bendigo's supporters, travelling from Nottingham, and Paddock's, from London. In fact this was not really the case, as the Nottingham people had to change trains

Figure 3.3   (*On facing page*) *Whitlingham Station near Norwich, with the Cathedral in the distance. Note the proud staff and the busy goods sidings*
Norwich Library

three times whilst Paddock's supporters came on a special train which left Bishopsgate at 8 am. Large numbers of third-class travellers from Nottingham were left to wait several hours in the middle of the night on Ely station – surely one of the most inhospitable places in East Anglia!

The special train from London had only first and second-class carriages, with fares of £2 and £1 return. 'Third class carriages were rejected to prevent the obtrusion of persons whose presence is invariably productive of disorder', it was reported. The first-class single fare to Ipswich, a somewhat shorter journey, was 15 shillings at about this time, so the 'special' mark-up was not too excessive.

Bendigo reached Mildenhall Road only after a difficult journey from Nottingham. He was nearly arrested and had to escape through some pig sties, then travelled by road via Stamford. He spent the night at Mildenhall Road's Railway Tavern, then went to the ring which was only a quarter of a mile from the station.

The fight lasted 49 rounds until Paddock was disqualified for hitting 'Bendy' after the ropes had broken and he had fallen to the ground. This so incensed 'Long Charley Smith' that he struck the referee's head wth a bludgeon. Paddock went back to London on the ECR train, nursing an injured right hand.

Another fight at Mildenhall Road ended in controversy in October 1851. The 'Championship of England' and 400 sovereigns were at stake, but the Tipton Slasher was disqualified after fouling Henry Broome. Again a special was run from London.

Surely the most extraordinary involvement of the ECR was with the fight on 10 May 1852 between Orme and Jones for £200. A special train left Bishopsgate (renamed from Shoreditch on 27 July 1846) just after 8 am with a number of fight fans who believed they were only going as far as Chesterford. However they only stopped there to water the engine, proceeding forwards along the old Newmarket line (officially closed from October 1851!) to Six Mile Bottom. Orme was meant to be waiting there, but he had got wind of Police activity and so the

special train (with ECR officials aboard) continued along the railway to Newmarket.

At this point accounts of the event vary. It seems that Orme met the train at Newmarket, from where he piloted it back along the disused line to Bourne Bridge, having lost some of the spectators along the way. One source even suggests that Orme gave directions while sitting on the tender. At Bourne Bridge fighting started at last, but they had only reached Round 9 when the cry of 'Peelers!' went up. In the resulting furore, everyone could be seen 'making for the train and jumping into the first carriage he could find.'

The train reversed direction once more and everyone travelled to Warren Heath, just beyond Newmarket, where a further 23 rounds were possible before another Police intervention. So it was back to the train once more, Orme still giving directions from the tender. They travelled along the old line again, passing a detachment of Police who were waiting at Six Mile Bottom. They rejoined the main Cambridge to London line and continued to a point two miles south of Chesterford.

Jones, rather than the Police, spoilt the proceedings this time. He said that he had thought the fight was abandoned and had therefore consumed some oranges and brandy while on the train. It may simply be that Jones had lost patience with this bizarre farce, as other reports say that he refused to get out of the train a third time. It was also said that the referee had resigned. But what did the Board of Trade think about such unscheduled use of a line 'which was at that time closed for general traffic'?

Arguably a point in favour of the ECR was that it did assist fight organisers in trying to keep out any likely troublemakers. However, the policy for doing this involved a blanket ban on the lower classes by pricing them out. For the April 1853 fight between Broome and Orme, the ECR laid on an 8.30 am special

Figure 3.4 *(On facing page) Stowmarket in the late 1890s. Several long sidings have been constructed to serve the maltings which formerly depended upon the Navigation, while newer malthouses have been built beside the line. The notorious crossing over Stowupland Road can also be seen*   Ordnance Survey

train of 16 packed carriages, but helped to keep out the 'common Cheapsiders' who tried to get aboard at Bishopsgate.

This special made a stop at Bishop's Stortford to pick up Orme and also at Elsenham to collect Broome. Only at the latter stop was the driver told where the train was going; it was hoped that this secrecy would prevent undesirables reaching the scene of the fight in advance.

However even the best laid plans were likely to go wrong if the ECR was involved, and so it proved when the special train reached Ely. It was learnt that a large number of 'Cheapsiders' had gone up by an earlier 'Parliamentary' train, and by sending a pilot engine on ahead it was found that they had all gathered at the usual fight location of Mildenhall Road. The solution to this was for the special to steam straight through Mildenhall Road without stopping. Police were waiting at Lakenheath, so the spot eventually chosen for the fight was half-way between two stations, close to milepost 108. Broome was the victor, but so was the ECR – they had taken the fares from the 'Cheapsiders', then helped to deprive them of the spectacle!

18 October 1853 was the date for Langham v. Sayers, this time with local interest since Langham was from the Ram Inn at Cambridge. Another 8.30 am special was run from Bishopsgate to Lakenheath, where over 400 passengers got out and 'invaded and overran the little station.' Battle commenced in a field 200 yards from the station, with Langham the victor after 122 minutes. On the return journey to London £50 was collected for the defeated Sayers.

8.30 am from Bishopsgate seems to have been the standard time for these trains. On Valentine's Day 1854, Paddock met Poulson at Mildenhall Road in a distinctly unloving confrontation. The special reached there at 11.15 am, giving plenty of time before the fight started at 12.30. Battle lasted 102 rounds, until 2.40 pm. For the last three rounds Poulson was blinded and eventually cried 'enough', whereupon Benjamin Caunt leapt into the ring and tried to continue. Poulson's head was 'beaten almost to a pulp', the *Cambridge Chronicle* claimed with a degree of artistic licence.

The 8.30 am from Bishopsgate brought over 1,000 to Mildenhall Road again on 26 June 1855 for Paddock v. Jones, with another fight between Mace and Slack occurring on 2 October 1855 in the same place.

By 1856 the authorities were getting wise to the habits of the pugilists, so a change of route was necessary. For the May 1856 fight between Paddock and Broome the ECR seems to have plotted with the organisers to evade the forces of law and order.

A special train was again arranged but filled up so rapidly at Bishopsgate that another seven carriages were added. Then some more gentlemen arrived and chose to charter their own special of four or five carriages; the passengers were said to include an Indian prince. The main special left at 9.15 am and stopped at Stratford to collect Broome. Halts for water were made at Chelmsford and Manningtree, and at the latter point 'intelligence' was received that the Ipswich Police were on the alert. Perhaps inspired by Napoleonic strategy, the pugilists decided to hold their fight as near to Ipswich as possible since that was where the Police would least expect them. The location of the fight was probably somewhere along Belstead Bank or beside the marshes south of Ipswich, and Paddock won in 51 rounds.

10 March 1858 saw huge crowds at Bishopsgate, but boxer Mace failed to arrive and so the special train was cancelled. Mace, who came from Norfolk, had a bad reputation for this sort of thing. A journalist used his time by making a pen portrait of a typical pugilism fan: 'He was buttoned up to the chin, in an old fashioned drab box-coat, with a deep red neckerchief, and a sealskin cap, the ears of which completely covered his ears and cheeks.'

By late 1859 the prize-fight traffic had begun to desert the ECR for the South Eastern Railway, whose open support of the practice led to debates in Parliament. It is now difficult for us to believe that a major Company like the ECR, with several MPs among its shareholders, made so much money over a long period through encouraging illegal activities! Railways were banned from carrying this traffic by a new law of 1868.

3.2 Holiday and Leisure Traffic

As the prize-fight issue shows, the ECR revealed early a tendency to make money out of unlikely passenger traffic. One other such occasion was the huge public interest shown in the Stanfield Hall murders of 1849, which resulted in the execution of the murderer Rush in Norwich. A large number of 'penny dreadfuls' sensationalised the case, and an excursion to the execution was run by the ECR from London. This train was halted at Wymondham to allow Police to prevent any further troublemakers going to Norwich that day. They had received warning of the excursion by telegraph – an early example of what was to prove a potent tool in the struggle for public order, first used by the GWR in 1843. Executions tended to attract pickpockets and the like; no more were required in Norwich!

Some much less morbid but far more enterprising excursions were organised at quite early dates. One of the earliest excursions ran on 20 September 1845 from Cambridge to Yarmouth, attracting over 500 passengers. The *Cambridge Chronicle* reported that 'soon after six o'clock on Saturday morning, crowds might have been seen wending their way to the station, and when the doors were thrown open, the crush for tickets was almost overpowering.'

Many trains were run for the Great Exhibition of 1851, but by then the ECR had already begun to widen its ambitions. An excursion from London to Rotterdam via Yarmouth was put on in July 1846, largely as a trial. The special train left Shoreditch at 5 am on a Thursday, connecting with the sailing of the steamer *Norfolk* at 9.50 am. Sadly the North Sea passage was very rough, with 'the sufferings of the majority on board [being] truly distressing.' The brass band's rendition of 'Rule Britannia' was cut short by a sudden onset of nausea, then strong winds blew the vessel so far off course that it did not reach Rotterdam until 10 am the next day. The excursion was not seen as a conspicuous success.

Thomas Cook was also providing imaginative excursions, often with an emphasis on education and no alcohol. Connec-

tions to many Cook excursions were possible via Peterborough. In August 1854 people from Cambridge went on an excursion to Edinburgh, with an all-inclusive charge of £1 14s 6d.

By the late 1850s many coastal towns were becoming keenly aware of the link between rail services and prosperity. In June 1861 the Lowestoft authorities complained bitterly that a dispute between the ECR and the Great Northern had brought a sudden halt to valuable excursion traffic from the Midlands. Things were made even worse by the lack of through trains to London, a change at Beccles being needed.

Excursions were run on virtually any pretext, such as the 1854 trip which brought 300 people from Hitchin for a tour around Cambridge. In September 1861 a train ran from Chatteris to Peterborough for a brass band contest. A party of young men and women from the former town made use of this service, though they seem to have had romantic rather than musical motives. The *Cambridge Chronicle* reported that on the return

Figure 3.5 *A view of Clacton-on-sea Station after the arrival of one of the late Victorian excursions that changed the face of the once rural village* Essex Libraries

journey, 'whether from forgetfulness of where they were, or whether it was that they were so charmed with each other's company' they missed their station and carried on to Somersham. They had to walk six miles home late at night: '. . . whether this mistake was an addition to their day's pleasure or not we are not in a position to say.'

Some excursion trains assumed mammoth proportions. The excursion from Cambridge to London on Whit Monday 1848 attracted so many passengers that it had to be run in two sections of 47 and 30 carriages respectively. An August 1861 excursion from Cambridge to Yarmouth mustered 1,304 passengers.

Figure 3.6 *Bury St Edmunds, Northgate Station, around 1900*

Suffolk Record Office

The GER ran regular excursions to Yarmouth and Lowestoft which were often pre-booked. With holidays so few, excursionists had to take a chance on the weather and at Easter 1874 they were greeted by a 'rather biting wind' at Yarmouth. None the less many went to the beach at both Yarmouth and Lowestoft, though some spread out into the countryside. In the evening St Olave's and Belton stations were both busy with returning excursionists.

In September 1874 a special was run to Yarmouth for the Races. On the return journey a number of excursionists arrived at the various stations too early for the train and found themselves in need of 'refreshment'. The hungry and thirsty excursionists made unwelcome visits to several nearby houses from which they removed 'eatables, drinkables, cups, saucers, tea, coffee, etc.' These spoils of war were taken off to the train, following which the day trippers threw the plates and cups out at stations they passed on the way home.

The opening of the Great Northern & Great Eastern Joint Line made a whole new programme of excursions possible. Thus in September 1882 the GER was advertising trips to Doncaster for the St Leger and to market day at Sleaford; one doubts if the latter produced huge crowds. Other trips being advertised at the same time included Cambridge and Haverhill to Harwich, St Ives and Newmarket to Harwich, and Saffron Walden and Cambridge to Yarmouth.

Some more adventurous excursions followed the trend set by Thomas Cook. Many poorer people could not afford a 'holiday' as such, but could manage an extended day out. To cater for this traffic the GER ran a series of excursions to Manchester in October 1882. Four separate trains were run, two starting from Norwich and one each from Ipswich and Cambridge, picking up more passengers en route. The main Norwich train had 800 passengers, and a total of 3,400 were carried in all. Those who travelled had to be quite hardy characters since the train from Cambridge left at 3.30 am, picking up 150 extra passengers from Ely at 4 am. A total travelling time of fourteen hours was involved for the Ely passengers who got home at 5.30 am the following day – it must have been later still for the Norwich contingent. The *Cambridge Chronicle* reported that 'Those who ventured on this memorable expedition speak in high terms of the pleasures of the day, and the tedium of the night.'

The employees of Bass & Co. the Burton brewers, were regular excursionists. On a number of occasions they organised mammoth excursions to Yarmouth, such as that of 25 July 1913. Fourteen special trains were organised to convey 8,000 people from Burton and another train brought in 400 of the London staff. About 230 carriages were needed, and the trains left Burton at approximately ten-minute intervals between 3.45 am and 6 am.

At Peterborough the engines were changed to GER ones and the manager of a nearby hotel provided refreshments. At Yarmouth the excursionists had to be handled without impeding the normal traffic, and each train was cleared and shunted in two minutes. Every available piece of track in the station area was used to store the empty carriages.

The return trains left Yarmouth between 7.35 pm and 9.45 pm in the same order as they had arrived that morning. However a number of people elected to stay on in Yarmouth and two further specials were needed on 1 August.

The years before World War I were the heyday of the railway excursion and leisure traffic. Easter Thursday 1912 saw a vast exodus from Liverpool Street to the coast. The 11.45 am Yarmouth express had to be run in three portions and the 12 noon Hunstanton in two. Between 3.20 pm and 3.30 pm there were five coastal departures to Cromer (2), Yarmouth (2), and Clacton. The 5 pm Yarmouth train ran in three portions with one going fast to Ipswich and Beccles. To cater for demand during the day, roads 9a and 10a at Liverpool Street were used to store spare carriages. These were certainly needed, for there would normally have been 16 main-line departures between 10 am and 5.15 pm, but instead there were 33. These were made up of five 12-wheel carriages, 170 8-wheel, 300 6-wheel, and even two 4-wheel.

Almost comparable to this in intensity was the football traffic.

The GER was involved with people travelling to matches at Tottenham, Clapton Orient, Woolwich Arsenal (Plumstead), Leyton, West Ham, Norwich, and Southend. Ipswich, Colchester, and Cambridge United were not then Football League clubs.

The most popular of these clubs was Spurs, who regularly attracted crowds of 40,000 in the pre-1914 days. Many spectators came by train, so before a match the size of the crowd would be calculated by the GER and the club. One of the greatest problems was what to do with the empty carriages while a match was being played.

For Spurs games, cheap tickets were issued to Park (later Northumberland Park) station from the Hertford line stations and other stations in the area as far as Broxbourne. Special trains from Liverpool Street usually ran non-stop to White Hart Lane or Bruce Grove. Other trains were sent forward half full to collect at intermediate stations.

The stationmaster at White Hart Lane was supported by extra inspectors on match days, and an extra entrance was built to assist with the flow of people. The returning fans were lined up by mounted Police and special trains were brought in from the sidings if no ordinary train was due. The gates of the station were closed every five minutes to prevent overcrowding of the platforms. If the number of passengers outstripped the supply of trains, then extras could be sumoned from Enfield Town or Liverpool Street. It was not unknown for there to be over 15,000 passengers per hour after a cup tie.

For Leyton games the cheap tickets were available from the Southend, Colchester, and Ongar lines. For Norwich it was possible to get half-day excursions from Ipswich, Yarmouth, Wells, Lowestoft, and King's Lynn.

Throughout Britain there were several lines built purely to encourage excursion and leisure traffic to coastal resorts. The best example of this on the GER system was the former Tendring Hundred Railway in Essex, built to link the Norwich main line with the coast at Walton-on-the-Naze.

This line was proposed in the early 1860s as an extension of a branch then being built to Wivenhoe, Walton being considered 'a well-known and favourite watering-place . . . a town annually resorted to by thousands.'

Such was the desire to build a railway to Walton, and so great the imagined profits, that for a time there were actually two lines to the small resort under construction. The second was the Mistley, Thorpe and Walton Railway, intended to bring in holiday-making hordes from the cities of the North via Ipswich. After making its claim to history by staging the famous Mistley railway riot, in which the contractor's men fought a pitched battle with hardened characters hired by the Railway, this scheme subsided into financial disaster.

Railway and property development tended to go hand-in-hand, hence a whiff of scandal that affected the early days of the Tendring line. Peter Bruff, engineer to the THR and former employee of the ECR, also happened to own land at Walton. Thus he could hope to profit from increased land values if the line was built, but the local press soon discovered that his involvement went rather deeper than that. It was revealed that the THR was buying land for its Walton terminus from Bruff and for its terminus at St Botolph's, Colchester, from its own Chairman. To make matters worse the Walton land was known to be unstable due to the actions of the sea and useless for housing development. 'Do not parts of that property sometimes go to sea? And do they ever return?' a correspondent asked in the *Essex Standard*. The implication was that the shareholders of the THR were being duped by Bruff, who had some useless land to dispose of.

The smell of scandal permeated the air by January 1863. Meeting at the Black Boy in Weeley, Bruff tried to justify the plan to use his Walton land:

> Mr Bruff exhibited his plan for carrying the railway along the cliffs at Walton, and explained that by intercepting the land springs, taking off the top weight, and putting it at the foot, so as to prevent the sea from sapping the base, he should have no doubt whatever of the stability of the line; it would be a means of keeping Walton where it is.

The Tendring Hundred Railway as saviour of Walton, indeed!

In fact he was wrong, for the soft cliffs at Walton still continue to give problems to this day, and Bruff's railway was no more exempt from natural forces than the houses built on the cliff. Though Walton station has retained its position, nearly a mile of the line had to be relaid in 1929 due to crumbling of the cliff.

Having secured his Walton line, though, Bruff went on to become engineer for the branch line to Clacton opened in 1882. This line also experienced problems, with wet weather and 'bad soil' delaying the opening. In fact Clacton benefited more from the post-railway development than Walton; its population more than trebled in the twenty years after the railway opened and it is now, of course, the main terminus of the Tendring line.

3.3 The Newmarket Traffic

Race traffic was responsible for the initial construction of a railway to Newmarket, albeit one that was soon exposed to harsh commercial reality when it had to abandon its direct link with the Cambridge to London main line at Great Chesterford. Thus the Newmarket and Chesterford line probably qualifies as East Anglia's earliest disused railway since regular trains ceased in 1851. Early in the present century there was a campaign by Royalty (the mistress-by-royal-appointment, Lily Langtry, had a house near the town) and others to get it reopened, but GER trains all continued to reach Newmarket via Cambridge if they came from London. Some of the earthworks of this line do remain, and its course is given away by a line of trees and a chalky mark across the fields.

Race traffic to Newmarket tended to be very exclusive since the Jockey Club did not actually welcome the attendance of the lower orders at the meetings. For many years the GER handled the traffic with some difficulty, since the old station there was a terminus into which trains often had to reverse, though it did have an associated platform on the through line. On 7 April 1902, though, the GER opened a new £40,000 station. The old station was retained for horse traffic and occasional excursions until at least 1954, with the capacity to handle 75 horse-boxes at a time. It was demolished in 1981, in spite of being a listed building.

The other station serving the Newmarket race traffic was at Warren Hill, beyond the tunnel that took the line beneath the Heath, and this was used solely for Race specials to and from the North. It consisted of an island platform with small offices.

1908 saw a considerable increase in the Newmarket traffic since the Jockey Club at last took steps to encourage third-class spectators by approaching the GER to run cheap excursions. This was seen as an attempt to compete with other racecourses nearer London.

Day trips were organised from Liverpool Street or St Pancras for 6s 6d return, though the still considerable number of first-class travellers could buy special season tickets to cover travel

Figure 3.7 *A very early photograph of Thetford Station, probably from the 1870s. Compare Figure 2.6 some 30 years earlier* Norwich Library

Figure 3.8 *The 5.20 pm goods to Cambridge passes through the new station at Newmarket on 4 August 1909, hauled by Type N31 No. 547* LCGB K. Nunn Coll.

to all major meetings during the year. They had their own exclusive trains too, including the 10.55 am from St Pancras. The busiest times were at the end of major meetings, when trains left for London at 4.10 pm, 4.18 pm, 4.30 pm and 4.50 pm. There were also trains from Warren Hill at 4.28 pm to Lincoln, Leeds, and Manchester, and at 4.35 pm to Peterborough. There could be over 6,000 passengers a day, as in 1907 when on one day 1,032 first-class and 3,659 third-class left for London, whilst 1,641 of both classes departed from Warren Hill.

To cope with the sudden surges in traffic the platforms at Newmarket station were each long enough to accommodate two trains. The platforms were also unique in being divided socially – 'ordinary' (first-class) passengers used one, and 'excursion' passengers (third-class) the other. (Second-class was abolished on the GER in about 1905, except in the London suburban area.)

Throughout the year there was also a steady traffic in horses, plus occasional busy periods during the bloodstock sales when the first-class traffic was again buoyant. Horses and their attendants were sent regularly to other race meetings around the country, 25 owners having their own private horse-boxes for this purpose. Traffic to race meetings at Derby in 1907 involved moving 209 horses and 407 attendants via Sleaford, with 197 horses going to the meetings at Liverpool with 240 attendants.

3.4 Goods Traffic

Animal traffic featured a great deal in the affairs of the GER and its ancestors. We have just read about the traffic in race-horses, but the range of creatures carried varied from turkeys to bulls. Sometimes the railway could represent a virtual moving abattoir and in October 1853 Six Mile Bottom certainly had the appearance of a kind of mortuary. The reason was that Colonel Hall and his friends had been shooting at Westley Bottom, as a result of which they despatched 1½ tons of hares and partridges to the London markets. At least this traffic was legal – a good number of East Anglia's poachers also sent their kills up to London by Great Eastern!

More unusual traffic of this sort turned up at Cambridge station in 1862 in the shape of a bag addressed to Mr Norton of Woodbridge. It was unclaimed at Woodbridge and so sent to the Post Office at Bishopsgate via a circuitous route. At Bishopsgate is was opened and found to contain the corpse of a child.

More lively traffic was evident at Thetford in May 1853. An infuriated bull, destined for Smithfield, made a desperate bid for freedom by breaking out of the station yard and setting off along the line to Brandon – the right direction for Smithfield.

A number of people chased the animal, some of whom were injured when the bull turned on its pursuers, and it was peppered with smallshot before this unusual 'working' was brought to its final terminus by a well-armed local gamekeeper.

In 1871 the GER was sued by a Mr Beldam for the cost of a cow which met an untimely end while in the care of the GER. On 21 January 1871 Beldam had loaded two cows, four steers, and a bull onto a goods train at Wisbech for delivery to St Ives market. The train should have reached St Ives by 8 pm, but did not in fact arrive until after midnight. This was not the crucial failure, however: the GER staff had put the bull into the same truck as the cows, securing it with the traditional ring through the nose. At some stage before the train reached Chatteris, the ring broke and the bull knocked down one of the cows, trampling it. When the train reached Chatteris the guard saw what had happened but did nothing about it, presumably being afraid to tackle the bull. By the time the train lumbered into St Ives, the cow was dead. The verdict went against the GER: an isolated incident which tells us a lot about goods practices of the time.

A cattle train was derailed between Newmarket and Kennett in December 1874, with three bullocks being killed. The train was also conveying drovers and cattle dealers, who had accompanied their animals on the long journey from Ireland.

Occasionally customers tried to defraud the GER over goods traffic, generally over the differential rates charged on various types of goods. In 1874 a respectable Lowestoft grocer, Adam Adams, was charged with defrauding the GER by sending a load of biscuit boxes as empties when they were in fact full. The biscuits were being returned to Peek, Frean & Co. as they were broken, the difference in rate between full boxes and empty ones being 11d. The case against Adams was dismissed on the grounds that he had sent off a large number of consignments that day and may simply have made a mistake.

An unusual dispute over goods traffic arose during the coal strike of 1890. The GER normally received its own coal supplies in daily deliveries to Hexthorpe Junction, near Doncaster, via the Manchester, Sheffield & Lincolnshire Railway. Once the coal strike began this supply dried up, but the GER knew there were thirteen trucks of its coal still in the sidings at Hexthorpe. It concluded that the MSLR was retaining this coal for its own purposes since it had also cut off supplies to the Great Northern. The platelayers at Hexthorpe had been instructed by the MSLR to remove the points so that the GER could not take the coal away by itself! In March 1890 the GER obtained an injunction, allowing it to take possession of its own coal.

The April 1917 edition of the *Great Eastern Railway Magazine* (known as 'GERM' to its friends) reported an unusual goods traffic that had commenced in June 1880. This was the delivery of good sea-water from Lowestoft to London, deliveries often amounting to 2,000 barrels a day, some of which went to London Zoo. It was claimed that a small eel was brought in one delivery and grew to a good size at the Zoo.

The traffic may have been due to a fashion for sea-water baths; the GER would deliver consignments of sea-water to any station for 6d per three gallons in special kegs. 'The kegs containing the water are perfectly tight, well-corked, and fitted with a handle, to admit of their being easily carried upstairs.' Deliveries of twelve gallons minimum were made in London at 1½d a gallon.

With so many connections to the east coast, the ECR and GER enjoyed buoyant fish traffic for many years. There were a number of disputes with fish merchants over this premium traffic, for its highly perishable nature made prompt delivery a necessity. The ECR did its best, as in August 1857 when it sent Mr Sweeting's oysters by passenger train from Maldon to London during warm weather, fixing the rate later – 1s 6d per hundredweight, plus 6d per package delivery.

In June 1861 there was a stormy meeting in Lowestoft since the railway had altered its train times, inconveniencing the traders. The traders also felt that better tramway links to the harbour were needed. By 1874 the traffic to London had grown to 27,046 tons, most of it using the East Suffolk line which had been completed in 1859.

Another type of freight traffic to the London markets was in

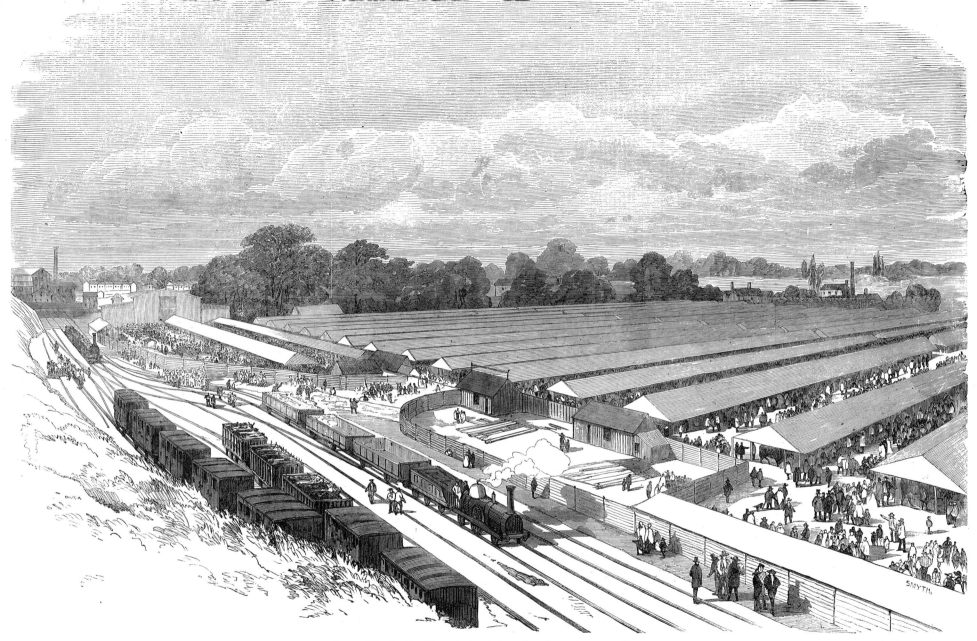

Figure 3.9   *Fashionable agricultural shows brought much extra traffic to the ECR,*
as this view of the 1856 Royal Agricultural Society Show at Chelmsford demonstrates
Illustrated London News, 19 July 1856

44

fresh peas. In 1880 the GER carried 5,887 tons of peas, though a problem with this traffic was that it was highly seasonal. Between 14 June and 6 August 1881 3,407 tons were delivered, with a record 450 tons being delivered to various places before 8.30 am on 9 July. In July 1898 the GER loaded 500 tons of peas in one day from stations in the Maldon area.

The GER served few industrial areas, but at Whittlesea and Peterborough its line passed through the middle of the brick pits. In 1891 the GER loaded 7,130 tons of bricks at Whittlesea, but the traffic grew rapidly and had reached 108,000 tons per year in 1898, when 23,000 tons of coal were also brought in to serve the brick kilns.

Earlier, the GER had been so keen to foster industrial traffic that in 1864 it placed a contract for the construction of a two-mile branch from the Ely to Norwich line to a brickworks at Shrub Hill, on Feltwell Fen. The line, in use by 1867 but closed by the early 1880s, was notable for its motive power. Two of the light locomotives were used, No. 17 (formerly *Ariel's Girdle*) and *Cambridge*.

On 19 June 1912 an important meeting was held in the Agricultural Hall, Norwich. The depression in farming was discussed and it was decided to develop the sugar beet industry to provide a new market for farmers. Cantley was chosen as the site for a sugar refinery, being close to both rail and water transport, and this opened later in 1912. A whole series of refineries was developed close to various GER lines at locations like Felsted and Ely. This, however, was yet another seasonal traffic.

In the 1890s traffic in jam and preserved fruit from the Chivers factory at Histon, near Cambridge, increased rapidly. In 1894 the non-coal goods traffic handled at Histon had been 10,546 tons, but this increased to 20,099 tons in 1898, 90 per cent in preserved fruit. Chivers paid the GER £12,294 in 1898.

The associated freight activity kept Histon station busy from 5.25 am to 10.50 pm each day, with several GER clerks handling all the paperwork. In the busy season there could be as many as six daily goods trains, bringing in sugar from Amsterdam and Hamburg, glass or earthenware pots from St Helens or Newcastle, and coal.

Each day about five laden trucks were sent to Bishopsgate goods terminal, three to Cambridge for trans-shipment, and two more each to Whitemoor, Norwich, Peterborough, Kettering, and Leicester. A recent introduction in 1899 was the 6.20 pm special goods which provided connections with the overnight express freight to Scotland.

During the fruit-picking season large numbers of Cambridge women were employed. These were ferried in and out on the 8.20 am and 6.34 pm trains at special rates.

A number of other places on the GER generated fruit traffic. Elsenham was also famous, Kelvedon handled the traffic from Tiptree, and there was also fruit grown in Suffolk north-east of Ipswich.

The ECR and GER did their best to encourage all such agricultural traffic for, unlike many other railways, there was no rich traffic in coal. The ECR was the first railway to convey fresh milk regularly into London, starting from Brentwood and Romford in about 1845. Some stations seemed to exist almost solely to serve the agricultural community, such as Cold Norton which was on the branch from Woodham Ferris (renamed Woodham Ferrers in 1913) to Maldon which opened in 1889.

It was a simple station consisting of one platform with gabled buildings on the west (down) side and a small goods yard with cattle dock adjacent. On the up side was a passing loop, seemingly for goods trains only, as there was no up platform, all guarded by a signalbox.

There was a large farmhouse called Flambard's two miles west of the station, and in the years immediately preceding World War I it was devoted to dairy cattle. It is interesting to see the connections between the farm and the station. First, and most obviously, the milk produced was taken to the station twice daily by pony cart. The pony knew the way very well, but for the sake of appearances any person at the farm who happened to be spare was sent along to accompany it.

Another important connection was due to the fact that the

well at the farm had long before dried up, so Flambard's had no drinking water. By a happy coincidence, the railway station had a plentiful supply, so a churn was filled up for the pony's return journey.

The third link between the farm and the station was not so vital as those noted above, but it was important for the budget of the farmer. Mr Todd was an excellent hand with a shot-gun, and could be relied upon to bag a rabbit with every cartridge. A cartridge cost 1d whilst an average rabbit fetched 10d or even a shilling for a good-sized one. The farmer had a friend who worked at the Stratford locomotive works, and there was little difficulty in crating up the rabbits and sending them up to Stratford by train, where there was a large and ready market for them.

Yet there were few passengers at Cold Norton and the line on which it stood was a failure; no doubt even Flambard's soon began to use the motor lorry instead of the train and on 10 September 1939 the station lost its passenger trains to be followed, on 1 April 1953, by the loss of its freight facilities too.

No time of year produced more colourful, varied, and chaotic freight traffic than Christmas. In its early days the ECR tried to handle both the heavy rush of passenger traffic, and a surge in the Norfolk turkey trade, through its one Shoreditch station. At Christmas 1846 Shoreditch station 'presented an unusual scene' on the Eve of the big day, according to the *Essex Standard*. Many trains arrived, 'containing a most extraordinary supply of poultry for the London market', and there were over 2,000 special packages of this sort on the morning mail train alone. So heavy was this traffic that the area in front of Shoreditch station was covered over with a tarpaulin and staffed with clerks whose special duty was to attend to the turkey traffic. In the midst of all these flying turkeys, passengers continued to pour in; a special afternoon train had to be put on to carry about 400 extra passengers in 30 carriages hauled by two locomotives.

Traffic had increased still further by the following Christmas. In one week in December 1847 the ECR handled 7,447 sacks of flour, 11,546 sacks of malt, 3,198 sacks of wheat, 3,414 sacks of barley, 1,374 sacks of oats, 1,052 sacks of seeds, 353 tons of meat, 193 tons of fish, 94 tons of poultry and game, 133 tons of beer, 5,594 sheep, 545 oxen, 181 pigs, 10,600 quarts of milk, 2,400 loaves, and 480 tons of coal. All that was missing was the partridge and the pear tree.

The following year the balance of traffic had altered slightly. 10,100 quarts of milk were carried and 8,000 sheep.

The list of deliveries for a week at Christmas 1861 gives us a good idea of the fashion in eating at the Victorian festive season: 1,498 oxen, 9,247 sheep, 620 pigs, 181 calves, 6,641 turkeys, 3,468 geese, 1,561 ducks, 884 hares and pheasants, 2,308 barrels of oysters, 24 tons of oysters in bags, 357 tons of meat, 350 tons of poultry, 329 tons of fish, 495 tons of cheese, 1,368 boxes of oranges, 685 bags of nuts, 2,053 boxes of dried fruit, 150 boxes of almonds, 15,103 sacks of flour, 57,583 quarts of milk, and 4,129 casks of beer.

The people who secured all this traffic for the ECR or GER were the 'canvassers'. In 1911, A. C. Chauncy, a canvasser for twenty years, wrote his 'confessions' for the *GERM*. He admitted that much of his work was conducted in pubs, citing the occasion when he repaired to a hostelry for consolation after losing a contract, and there met a major manufacturer who eventually awarded him a large volume of traffic.

At an agricultural show he 'tossed' for some traffic against a rival canvasser and won three wagon loads for the Great Eastern. However he also once walked six miles to get a contract for an exhibitor's traffic to a show, only to discover that it amounted to one racing pigeon! On another occasion he nearly lost 250 tons to a waterway carrier, but a traction engine fell through a bridge and blocked the rival's route.

Chauncy also knew the passenger canvassers who tried to arrange excursions and block bookings. One of these was in a group of rivals who were trying to secure a 'load' of 600 sailors from London docks to Liverpool – hardly GER territory. However, in trying to explain how they would get there, the GER canvasser mentioned Liverpool Street; the Spanish captain, confused by all the arguing Englishmen, seized on the name of the station since it sounded just what he wanted and booked to go Great Eastern. Presumably they travelled along the 'Joint' line via March and Lincoln to get to Liverpool, but there can't have been many London to Liverpool travellers who went by GER.

Figure 3.10 *Whittlesea Station*   Cambridgeshire Libraries

4

The Human Factor

4.1 Life on the Line

The one thing that can be said with certainty about life for the early railway workers was that it often tended to be short. Many navvies were killed during the construction of East Anglia's railways, whilst numerous railway employees suffered the same fate.

Many accidents were simply due to dangerous or careless practices. Two 'ballastmen' were killed near the ECR's Laken Heath station in January 1847. Joseph Roderham and William

Figure 4.1 *Proud locomotive men pose on T19 No. 708 at Colchester in November 1912*
LCGB K. Nunn Coll.

Talbot were rather foolishly riding on a ballast wagon when its front axle snapped. The following wagon mounted the one on which the two men were riding, crushing them. The Coroner's verdict was 'Accidental Death'.

The construction of the first railway to Newmarket resulted in a stream of navvies being brought into Cambridge for emergency treatment. The *Cambridge Chronicle* commented: 'A day seldom passes without some poor fellow being brought to the Hospital, either dismembered or in such a state that no human aid can avail to save him.'

It was not always just the lowly employees or construction workers who suffered. William Newall had been stationmaster at Ely for a while, but at the time of his unfortunate demise was manager of the Norfolk Division of the ECR. In April 1850 he had gone out with several other gentlemen on the *Eagle*, a curious hybrid of engine and carriage that is believed to have included the only railway locomotive ever built in Cambridge. They inspected the swing bridge at Haddiscoe, then returned to look at Reedham. There Newall jumped off while *Eagle* was still in motion, but his foot got caught and he was run over by the loco and its 'car'. The accident was fatal.

This was a common type of accident, but rare for a senior official. The same thing happened to a 'night man' when he got off a moving engine at Manea in 1852. His foot was crushed and had to be amputated.

Just how dangerous working on the railway could be was proved by the case of William Armstrong, aged 47. He was found dead on the line near Stratford in 1852, with an arm and a leg cut off. At the inquest the jury observed that the ashboxes of ECR locomotives were too low to allow reasonable chance of escape in the event of being knocked down. Armstrong was the last of eight workers who had joined the ECR from the

London & North Western Railway; all had been killed at work.

Most accidents of this sort occurred when workers ignored safety regulations. In the summer of 1854 two labourers were travelling by four-wheel trolley along the Somerleyton to Haddiscoe line. They had ignored the fact that a down train was due, so when the train came in sight of them its driver attempted to stop by frantically reversing his engine. The men jumped off the trolley and tried to get it off the line, but Jeremiah Jones was struck by the engine, 'mangling and tearing his limbs in a frightful manner.'

In June 1913 the *GERM* carried an account by a labourer who claimed to have been chased by an engine! The event is said to have occurred about 1880 when the man was working as a ganger on the line between Elmswell and Thurston in Suffolk. About 50 men were relaying track at a point where the line dipped, with rising gradients either side.

A down goods train came through at a considerable speed, but its ninth truck became derailed and the other wagons followed. The ganger went and stood between the tracks at the rear of the derailed train, whose trucks had splayed across the up line. Other gangers rushed forwards in a vain attempt to stop an oncoming up goods train.

The ganger stood motionless between the tracks, watching the up goods smashing its way through the derailed trucks of the down train. His colleagues fled for safety round behind the derailed train, but it was not until there were just a few seconds remaining that the ganger realised the advancing train was not going to stop before it reached the position he was standing in.

There was no time left to escape round the rear of the down train, so he crossed the up track and ran down the 'batter' (or embankment). As he did so the up engine reached the place where he had been standing and itself derailed, appearing to pursue him down the bank.

At the bottom of the bank was a wooden fence, and the desperate ganger attempted to vault it by putting his foot on the top rung. The fence snapped beneath him and he was thrown into the field, grazing his shin. Fortunately the run-away engine had slithered to a halt a few feet away from him

> . . . pouring her steam and water out of her funnel, howling, shrieking, and groaning, making the most unearthly noises I ever heard, just for all the world as if she were some huge living monster, cheated out of her intended prey, and dying with rage at the disappointment.

Not all near misses on the ECR and GER involved trains. At Longstanton in February 1861 the stationmaster and his wife were aroused from their sleep by a strange noise in their children's bedroom. They went through to the room to find that some bricks had fallen through the ceiling, injuring the face of one of the children. The parents got their children out of bed and they were just leaving the room when the entire chimney stack came crashing through onto the bed where the children had been sleeping minutes before. Their escape was reckoned to be miraculous.

Life was not always dangerous, and of course many men worked through their time to enjoy a happy retirement. Some became very popular with their local communities, like Robert Gibson, for nine years a humble crossing keeper at Adelaide Bridge near Ely. When he gave up this post local people rewarded him with a silver tobacco box because of the high quality of his services. When the stationmaster at Waterbeach retired in 1882 he was given a 'handsome gold watch' after a subscription had been raised in the district. Such cases show what an important part of local community life the railway was.

Not all stationmasters were so popular and it would seem that some were rather too busy on 'extra-curricular activities'. In 1890 the stationmaster at Woodham Ferrers was cited in a divorce case. He was named Avery and was the first stationmaster in the village on a newly-constructed line. As the station house was incomplete, he lodged with a local farmer for a while. The farmer became suspicious that something was going on between Avery and his wife when he returned home to find that the sofa had been moved. Also his wife often seemed 'flushed' after she had been with the stationmaster.

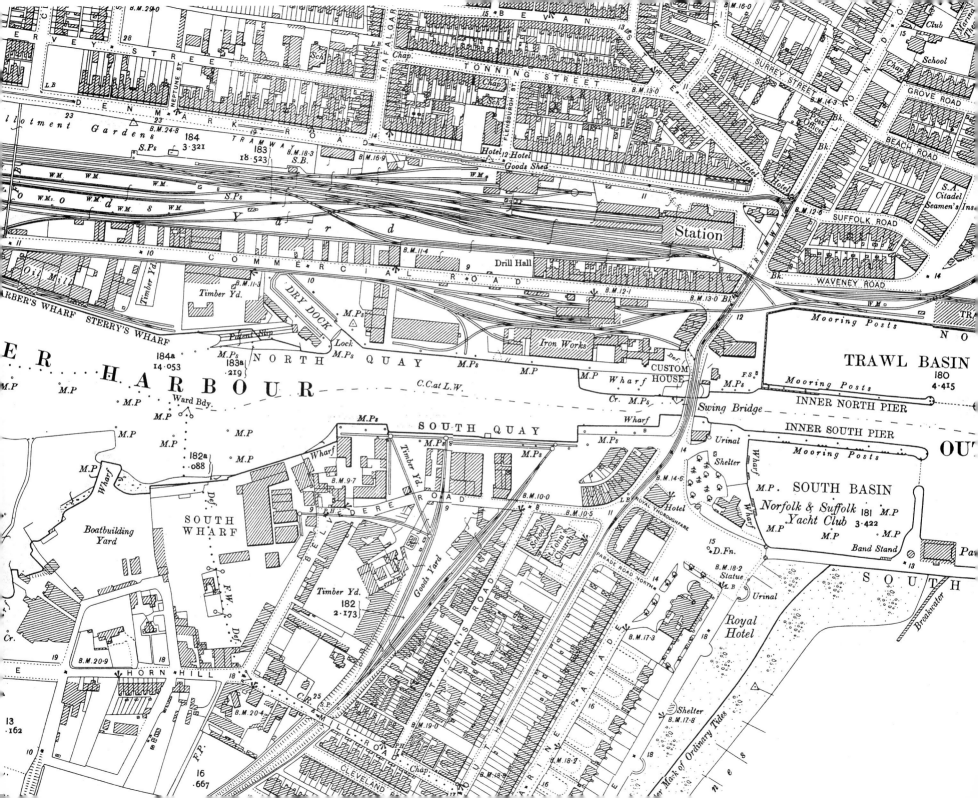

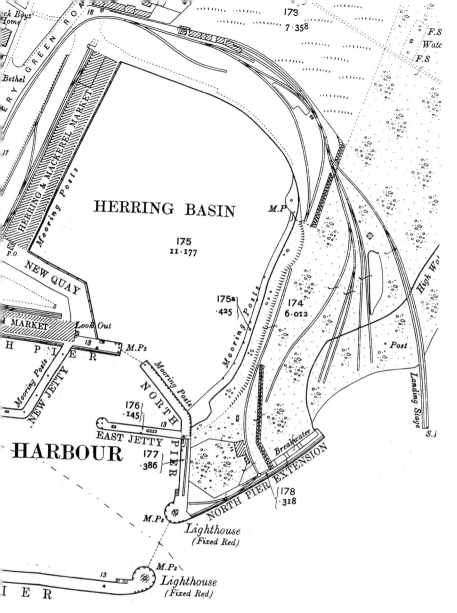

Figure 4.2 *Lowestoft in the 1890s. The impressive way in which the GER tried to cater for the fish traffic can be well seen: sidings serve all the wharves on both sides of the river as well as the fish markets by the harbour* Ordnance Survey

The couple were certainly quite active, because they made use of the spare bedroom when they thought that the farmer was asleep. Perhaps the most intriguing feature of the case is the considerable family responsibilities that the two guilty parties had – the farmer's wife had nine children and the stationmaster had seventeen! How these were all meant to fit into a GER station house remains a mystery.

A certain amount of mystery surrounds the activities of the 'Wicked Woman of Chigwell', who was said to be the wife of the Chigwell stationmaster. Quite which station in the area her husband was in command of remains uncertain, but the woman got involved in a scandal following her allegations against a local doctor called Saunders. The doctor was eventually proved

Figure 4.3 *On shunting duties beside the quays at Lowestoft in 1901, 0–4–0ST No. 229, Class 209* LCGB K. Nunn Coll.

to be innocent and the event was commemorated in a mid-Victorian ballad entitled the 'Wicked Woman of Chigwell'.

Come one and all and listen to
This funny little song
Concerning Mrs Harrison,
I will not keep you long;
She in Chigwell Road resided,
With her husband, so it's said,
She swore that Saunders on the 12th of March
Assaulted her in bed.

So listen to this funny tale
She tried to cause much strife
Did this false screaming woman,
The Chigwell stationmaster's wife.

At Epping Sessions, there this case occurred
And she said, now only think
That the doctor Mr Saunders
With her played at tiddly-wink;
Then he went into her chamber
When her husband left the room,
How far the story there was true
I'll let you know full soon.

She refused to say one word about
Her former course of life;
Oh, is she not a beauty,
This Chigwell stationmaster's wife.
Then the council [*sic*] for the doctor
Soon put this lady down,
By asking her the manner
She lived in Peterborough town.

Now a witness he was called,
And when he did pop in;
Pray do you know this gentleman?
She cried, yes, all serene;
But whether it is true or not,
At least the folks do say
That he with this famed Mrs Harrison,
Some funny games did play.

Round Ilford and round Epping
And Romford too it seems,
That she was very fond of pork
And she dearly loved her greens,
But to swear that Dr Saunders
Assaulted her, 'twixt me and you,
She must tell it to the devil
For with us that tale won't do.

One word for Doctor Saunders
That kind and skilful man,
She ought to be well bonneted,
And put in the prison van,
Such disgraceful dirty conduct,
It really was too bad,
And when the Doctor was discharged,
The people were right glad.

Figure 4.4 *The 11.50 am Lowestoft to Yarmouth goods sets off past Coke Ovens Junction in August 1912, hauled by S46 No. 1863* LCGB K. Nunn Coll.

Enquiries show that a Doctor Sanders lived in Chigwell Row in the late 1850s and early 1860s, so it seems possible that there is some truth to this ballad. However, no stationmaster named Harrison has yet been identified in the district at that time. The allegations about Mrs Harrison's activities in Peterborough sound quite libellous.

On a more straightforward subject, some families developed great loyalty to the Railway and worked on it for generations. Most famous were the Paige family, who between 14 of them amassed 349 years of service by 1912. The oldest member of the clan was F. Paige, who was stationmaster at Denver and North Wootton stations from 1854 to 1874; he was succeeded at North Wootton by E. G. Paige from 1874 to 1891 and F. A. Paige from 1900 to 1914.

The railway offered a good career structure for an ambitious young man, but it was also a huge organisation in which things could go wrong. Staff were disciplined frequently – for example, sending items of freight to the wrong destination would result in a small fine. Checker Hood was fined 1s in about 1893 for sending a bag of sugar to Colchester instead of Lynn whilst Assistant Loader Jones was 'cautioned' when two casks of jam meant for Great Bentley were delivered to Chelmsford. Checker Yeo sent a case of cocoa to Chelmsford instead of Chingford – at least he got the first two letters and the last syllable right! Checker Halls was fined a day's pay when he tried using an old rope to load a side of beef; the rope broke and the beef fell onto a carman.

Railwaymen had to work in all weathers; in the early years drivers and firemen were virtually unprotected from the elements while at work. At Spitalfields in London, arch No. 3 in Wheeler Street was known as the 'Cokemen's Lodge' and was used by ECR men to dry their clothes. Perhaps it was the drying of clothes that set it on fire in January 1847.

A relatively unsung group of railway workers were those who laboured in the GER laundry at Colchester. This was built in 1888 and was powered by a 35 hp Davey Paxman engine, made locally. It had to do all the washing for the Company's

MUDDLEBY JUNCTION

Overworked Pointsman (puzzled). " Let's see !—there's the ' scursion ' were due at 4.45, and it ain't in ; then, afore that, were the ' mineral,'—no ! that must ha' been the ' goods,'—or the ' cattle.' No ! that were after,— cattle's shunting now. Let's see !—fast train came through at—— Con-found !—and here comes ' the express ' afore its time, and blest if I know which line she's on ! ! "

Figure 4.5 Punch *took great pleasure in making fun of railway staff, though this hardly made travellers more confident!*

hotels, restaurant cars, and steamers. In 1890 949,030 articles were washed but by 1911 this had risen to 3,473,121, necessitating a staff of 59 girls and 12 men. 500 table napkins could be washed, starched, and ironed in an hour, but the heaviest task was when 700 blankets at a time were delivered from the steamboats. There was certainly no sex equality at the GER laundry – men and women had separate dining rooms.

It was often necessary for the train crews to sleep away from home and so the GER had its own dormitory at Stratford. This opened in 1890 and had 50 beds. An attendant was on duty 24 hours a day to cook meals. Each 'guest' was given clean sheets and a pair of slippers to use.

4.2 Staff in Trouble

Railway staff were frequently involved in crime, sometimes as its victim and sometimes as its cause.

Physical assault seems to have been fairly rare compared to the publicity it receives today. An exception to this was clearly Colchester station, where cab drivers had an uneasy relationship with railway staff. Richard Callaby, a cab driver, was twice fined £5 in the late 1840s for assaulting porters. On the second occasion he got into an argument about the rule whereby the first cab in the line took the first customer. Losing his temper, Callaby hit a porter in the face and then lashed out with a whip. He had to be pulled away by other ECR staff.

There was a bitter irony to a tale about an assault on a member of the railway staff at Ware. It was a busy time at the level-crossing there one day in January 1847, since a train had just left for Hertford and one was expected from Hertford at any moment. A man named Roe got impatient at waiting and attempted to cross the line. When the crossing keeper tried to stop him, Roe punched the man in the face. Seconds later Roe

WHEN IN DOUBT—DON'T!

SCENE—*Country Station*

Gent. "Are the sandwiches fresh, my boy?"
Country Youth. "Don't know, I'm sure, sir. I've only been here a fortnight!"

Figure 4.6 A Punch cartoon that, despite all the changes in railway travel, links the mid nineteenth with the late twentieth century in a topic of perennial debate

was knocked down by the up train and his legs were cut off just below the knees.

In February 1847 the staff at Shelford, near Cambridge, were troubled by three men who started begging. The stationmaster summoned the village Constable, whereupon both men were assaulted by the beggars. Somehow the three troublemakers were taken off to the lock-up for the night, but they escaped using a skeleton key!

Money and other valuables were often entrusted to staff; occasionally this was too much of a temptation. In March 1857 stationmaster Lines of Shelford was given twelve months in prison for embezzlement. The sentence was reduced due to good character testimonials being given for him.

It was rare for a senior official to abscond with money. However in 1853 the Ipswich stationmaster, Cole, did just that. Although paid a quite substantial £110 a year, Cole had come under suspicion of fiddling the books and decided to escape before he was arrested. He had all his furniture valued and sold in advance, but then ran off leaving his wife and child behind.

In 1860 a wages clerk, Algernon Lumby, absconded with at least £100. He disappeared in February 1860 and was believed to have gone abroad, a Police Superintendent even going to the continent to investigate. Lumby was arrested eventually at Scarborough under curious circumstances: he was working as a pianist at St George's Hall when he was recognised by a former friend who was on holiday. The Police were told and an officer approached Lumby between songs; they shook hands and the officer informed Lumby that he 'had come for him'. Lumby was allowed to finish his performance before being arrested.

In September 1874 two GER guards appeared in court at Bury charged with stealing three bottles of claret in August. The guards were in charge of a train where the load included a hamper for Elmswell, from which they removed the bottles. Two full bottles were found in the brake van's sand locker and the other was hidden beneath a coat. Staff were invariably sacked after such incidents.

A few months later a much larger operation was discovered. James Cutting, a GER platelayer based at Mildenhall Road, and William Barker, a former Brandon signalman, were charged with a variety of thefts. The first item on their rather curious list was 45 yards of carpet, valued at £11. This was en route from Halifax to Norwich and had been 'checked' at March, but it never reached its destination. When Cutting's cottage was searched he was found to have some of the carpet down in his living room. The rest of the carpet was found in Barker's rooms at Hyde, Cheshire, where he had moved after leaving the GER. Barker accused Cutting of being the thief. Also discovered in Cutting's cottage were 18 gallons of beer worth £1. The beer was hidden in the closet, Cutting claiming that he had found it 'in the grass'. Presumably it had 'dropped off the back of a train'.

Detailed investigation revealed a quantity of red flannel cloth, 320 yards of cashmere, a hamper containing 107 pairs of boots, five pieces of silk lustre, three dozen gross of thimbles, 40 lb. of white silk, and a Europe sewing machine, all in Cutting's possession. Most of this had been stolen at Brandon station. Perhaps Cutting was planning to set up as a textile merchant . . .

1874 was clearly a bad year for the staff of the GER, some of whom lacked a certain finesse when it came to customer relations. Stationmaster Chilvers of Flordon, on the Norwich and Ipswich line, was prosecuted for assault, having literally smashed in the teeth of a goods customer. The poor victim of this attack was Henry Smith, a coal merchant, who had gone down to Flordon sidings to ask if a consignment of coal had arrived. He was intercepted by Chilvers who demanded, 'What are you shacking about for, you dirty scoundrel?' He then man-handled Smith roughly, pushing him back against some trucks and hitting him three or four times until two teeth were broken. The assault only stopped when an express train approached. Chilvers claimed in defence that his beard had been pulled and that Smith was trespassing on part of the line not open to the public. He was fined £5.

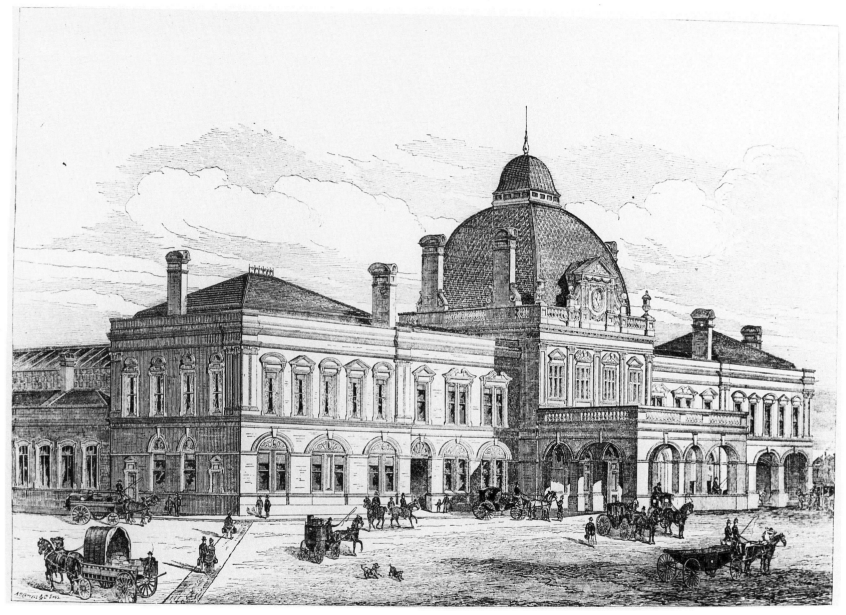

Figure 4.7   *The grand façade of the new Norwich Thorpe Station in 1886*
Norwich Library

56

A more unusual case still involved the East Anglian Hotel at King's Lynn in 1853. Staff of the ECR were in the habit of going to this pub for solid and liquid refreshment, although on Sundays they were not allowed to drink alcohol due to the licensing laws. On 8 May, a Sunday, the ECR Manager at Lynn sent six men, who had worked an overnight cattle train, to the Hotel for their breakfast. They had ale with their food but were interrupted by two policemen who saw the empty beer jugs. The landlord was fined 5s 6d.

A frequent problem in rural areas was that disaffected labourers or spurned beggars could take revenge on farmers by setting fire to barns or haystacks. Fire was not so easily used against a railway, but the same revenge motive was said to lie behind a horrific charge laid against Thomas Annison in 1851. Annison, it was alleged, had attempted to plunge a passenger train into the river at Reedham. Annison had been employed by the Norfolk Railway as an assistant at the Reedham swing bridge, where the bridge was often moved to allow the passage of wherries and other vessels. He was sacked for dishonesty, however, and only a few weeks later was implicated in an incident which could have cost many lives.

The Reedham bridge was subject to strict rules so as not to obstruct river navigation. The span was normally 'closed' to the railway, only being 'opened' five minutes before a train was due. Elaborate steps were therefore taken to keep trains off the bridge unless their approach was authorised. Two keepers looked after the bridge at a time, their principal duties at 'openings' being to 'pin' each end of the bridge and check the levels – which could be altered with a wrench if necessary. Having done this, one keeper was to walk away from the bridge in each direction to meet any train stopped at the signal posts on either side. Trains over the bridge were limited to 4 mph.

On the day of the near-disaster traffic was heavy and heavier-than-normal locomotives were being used. The bridge was prepared for a train expected at 6.10 pm and the keepers walked to either side in preparation. As the train drew onto the bridge there was a strange noise and 'great oscillation' of the loco-motive. It was found that one of the iron wrenches had been deliberately placed across the track in an attempt to wreck the train. Shortly after this Annison was seen nearby, and was arrested. At his trial, though, a verdict of 'Not Guilty' was returned as there was only suspicion against him and no solid evidence.

A curious tale with some similarities to this was told in the *East Anglian Magazine* in 1973. It concerned the station at Black Bank, between Ely and March. In about 1900 this was a lonely place indeed, the entire community consisting of the station, the signalbox, and about four houses in the middle of the Fens.

It was hardly the place for a career-minded fellow to be, and the stationmaster there was said to be so desperate to move that during the course of one plea he burst into tears. His situation contrasts with the case of a GER signalman who loved his home so much that he committed suicide rather than be transferred elsewhere by the Company. The Black Bank stationmaster was advised that promotion could only be based on merit, so it seemed that he was destined to watch Black Bank's four stopping trains a day until the end of his working life.

The stationmaster decided to bring himself to the attention of the GER hierarchy by dramatic means. He planned for an obstacle to be placed in the way of a train so that he could signal the danger and dramatically avoid disaster. Unwisely, perhaps, he told the porter of his plan, and the porter got into contact with the district Inspector.

The Inspector's advice seems rather curious – the porter should slip a dose of castor oil into the stationmaster's tea to prevent his foolish plan being carried out. This was done on the morning the deed was due to take place, the result being that the stationmaster was confined to bed until the doctor and a constable arrived. He was taken off to be certified and it was the porter who was rewarded with promotion!

4.3 Beside the Line

The life of many villages and towns were totally changed by

the opening of the railway, both socially and economically. Nowhere was this more so than at Stratford, which developed into a major railway junction and depot after the opening of the ECR. In 1912 William Wallis wrote to the *GERM* to record his impressions of life there 70 years earlier, soon after the first railways had been opened:

> My earliest recollections of the Eastern Counties Railway date from the years 1844–1845 when, as a boy of seven or eight, I was at all times clamorous for permission from my Mother to go and see the trains, for the railway, even then, had a peculiar attraction for me. It was my greatest delight to scamper across the Bread and Cheese fields, now the Stratford New Town, to the Angel Lane bridge, and scramble for a place on the granite coping which surmounted the brickwork of the original bridge at that spot, from which point of vantage myself and companions, boys of my own age or thereabouts, could get a good view of the railway and watch the incoming passenger trains and the shunting operations.
>
> The Stratford station booking office and platforms were close to the bridge. An old fellow on the platform dressed in a corduroy suit with a shiny cap (I don't remember seeing any other man in the shape of a porter there) used to go to a rope, whenever he expected a train (or it seemed so to us boys) and pull it, when it rang a little bell in the turret on the roof, when we immediately became on the alert. Then the train would make its appearance

in perhaps ten minutes or a quarter of an hour, with its groaning and squeaking noise and sulphurous smell from the engine. They always burnt coke then; of course the noise was occasioned by the pressure of the wooden brake-blocks on the tyres of the carriage wheels, but we did not know it then, and no-one could tell us, and we wondered at the cause, and then the guard would descend from his place on the roof of one of the carriages. He invariably had his eye on the passengers' luggage, for that was placed beside him on the roof too, covered with a tarpaulin or waterproof sheet.

> It often became a matter of controversy with us boys in forecasting our future as to which was the best job, and the most promising, the guard or the driver, for they both seemed very important personages, the guard with his greatcoat collar turned up above his ears and an oilskin cover to his cap or the driver who caused the train to move, and who stood in front of a roaring fire, but who had no other protection from the weather. At that time there used to arrive at Stratford on Saturday afternoons two or three cattle trains from the country, to be unloaded there in readiness for the old Smithfield market on Monday mornings. It used to delight us exceedingly to watch the unloading of them, especially the sheep.

Figure 4.8 *The huge new Stratford Works of the ECR in 1851. This factory opened in 1848 was the only major benefit to the ECR during the chairmanship of Hudson, the Railway King, and for some years Stratford was known as Hudson's Town*
ECR Guide, 1851

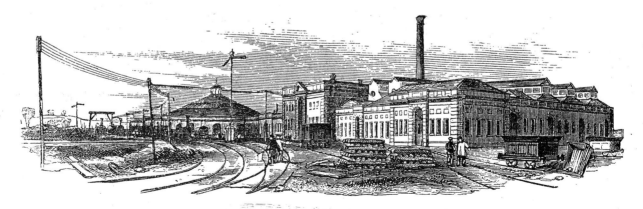

The railway changed Stratford very quickly and very thoroughly. Here is what the *Essex Standard* had to say about changes there in 1847:

> Few places exhibit more outward and visible signs of improvement than Stratford and West Ham. We have previously announced that at the former place a new railway town is in course of erection, comprising several hundred houses, numerous workshops and depots of various kinds, in addition to a new church; nor is this the only improvement: within the last few years several hundred houses have been built in the immediate vicinity, and as many are in course of erection, for the habitation of a population that is daily increasing, to add to the wealth, the importance, and the prosperity of that locality.

At Cambridge the railway was kept to the edge of the city and a clear social division emerged between those who lived on the opposite sides of the tracks. None the less the railway formed the focus of an unusual activity not normally associated with early railways – betting. This strange practice was explained in one of the Cambridge newspapers during 1845:

> The curiosity of our fellow townsmen in the humble walks of life seems as if it never would be sated. Night after night crowds of both sexes congregate in the vicinity of the railway station to watch the arrival and departure of the evening trains. About half-past-seven it is even betting between the up-train and the down-train which shall get first into the station, so the vacant ground on either side has its occupants, looking along the line for a curl of steam to herald the arrival. When the bell rings, those at the losing end run helter-skelter to the opposite end, and if they are lucky they get there just in time to see the monster pass them; and then away they all race off as fast as legs can carry them to see the departure, and most likely to gaze in the meantime upon a line of carriages, full of indignant passengers, doomed by the perverse ingenuity of somebody or other to wait within sight of port for some ten minutes or a quarter of an hour, until room is made for them by the getting away of the train which happens to monopolise the station. This is quite an exciting scene, and the up-train is backed against the down-train by speculative folks, just as they would back Lord Exeter against the Duke of Bedford upon Newmarket Heath.

Well, at least it made train-spotting more exciting. The curious situation was in part due to the fact that Cambridge station had one platform so that the trains had to take it in turns to call there.

4.4   The Strange Case of 'Mad' Windham

By the late 1850s the ECR had a bad name for safety and the general conduct of its affairs. In the early 1860s the Directors can hardly have believed that things could get worse – but they did. In 1861–2 the ECR was involved in a most sensational lunacy hearing that occupied the national press for week after week. Unfortunately a good deal of the evidence in the case centred upon murky activities aboard ECR trains!

At the centre of the case was an eccentric young aristocrat from Felbrigg Hall in Norfolk, W. F. Windham. A relative, Major-General Windham, brought an action for lunacy against him at the Court of Exchequer in Westminster. At the centre of the case was the question of who would inherit the family estates and a very considerable fortune, for young Windham had come under the influence of undesirables.

Even the 'trial' itself was something of a spectacle, with over 250 witnesses being called and an estimated cost of £160 per hour during the two months that it lasted. General Windham himself engaged a Counsel who charged 500 guineas down, plus £50 per day.

As a boy Windham was rather indulged by eccentric parents who, for example, allowed the young boy to dress up in the uniform of a servant. As the hearing developed, many servants were brought forward to explain the details of his early life. Then he had been sent to Eton where he had quickly acquired the nickname of 'Mad Windham', though his offences were rather minor – running up a bill of 18s for pastries, and eccentric behaviour.

It was once he had left school that Windham began to have more scope for his strange behaviour. He took lodgings in London with a Mr and Mrs Llewellin, who were key witnesses at the hearing. They gave colourful descriptions that weighed heavily against the young man, foremost among which was that he had paid his bills without looking at them! Windham was described as having 'very dirty habits', which included a 'disgusting' way of eating eggs. Despite this he apparently enjoyed baths; in the mornings he would have a cold bath followed by a very hot one, and then would walk about the Llewellin's house 'in a state of total nudity'. Doubtless the Romans would have thought him quite normal!

But the greatest amount of publicity centred upon Windham's activities on the ECR and the Eastern Union Railway in Norfolk, Suffolk, and Essex. The most harmless part of his obsession with railways was his delight in dressing up in the uniform of a railway servant and 'attending upon trains in a menial capacity'. This must have caused great consternation to the Victorians; they were very conscious of the social order, and no doubt felt confused by an aristocrat playing at being a worker. It was said that Windham liked to appear at wayside stations in a railway uniform, calling out, 'Get into your carriages, ladies and gentlemen.'

During summer 1861 he appeared at many wayside stations throughout East Anglia, generally causing a threat to the safety of passengers. At Haughley in Suffolk he started blowing a whistle on the platform, then he moved on to Stowmarket where he impersonated a guard so successfully that a train started too soon and several passengers fell out of the carriages they were getting into.

A few days later an Inspector of the EUR at Colchester was alerted by the frantic blowing of a locomotive whistle. He found Windham on the footplate of the stationary engine, having a great time. At the hearing, the Inspector gave evidence that 'I came to the conclusion that he was short in his intellect.' Maybe the Inspector thought Windham had escaped from the Essex Hall Asylum, which had been set up in the former Station Hotel just by the railway.

Money opened doors for young Windham, sometimes quite literally. He gained a set of EUR carriage keys for himself and bribed guards to allow him to travel in secluded compartments with young ladies of doubtful morality. This behaviour nearly caused apoplexy at the offices of the *Essex Standard*:

> Our readers, on seeing this evidence, how wild young men of property – and in this instance half idiot (at least) – are allowed to act as guards and engine-drivers, and to cause carriages to be locked for adulterous amours, will not be much at a loss to account for some of the many incidents and irregularities which from time to time have made the Eastern Counties Railway notorious.

Windham also bribed engine-drivers into letting him take charge; on several occasions he drove expresses between Colchester and Ipswich. This makes him sound like the king of an obscure Balkan state, who used to insist on driving the Orient Express where it passed through his kingdom.

Windham became friends with Joseph Ford, an ECR guard, and the two used to travel together when Ford was on duty. Windham normally brought gifts along with him – one time this involved three bottles of champagne and one of sherry, which Ford helped to consume. By January 1862 Ford was no longer a guard with the ECR, his employers being rather displeased with all the adverse publicity.

Windham was still a young man when his father died, an event which caused him great grief. Under the terms of the will he was to come into the estate at the age of 21, but he still had plenty of money to burn.

The combination of ready cash and nothing to do led Windham into some bizarre pursuits, such as acting as a private detective in Norwich and going around 'arresting' people. Witnesses at the hearing also testified that he drove a mail cart at 'furious speed' in the belief that he was at a circus. It was alleged that he ordered (and paid for) sumptuous banquets to which he issued no invitations and to which no one went – not even himself. At a dance he had threatened to box a young lady's ears as 'she did not dance well enough to please him.'

In 1861 Windham developed a far more dangerous passion

than trains – women. At Ascot he met an infamous courtesan named Agnes Willoughby, a woman who lived in fine style in Piccadilly at the expense of a merchant named Rogers. She also enjoyed the attentions of another lover named Roberts. These two set out to exploit Windham, starting off with getting him to buy Agnes £14,000 worth of jewellery.

General Windham returned from India to find his nephew in the clutches of the two worldly-wise characters, but there was little he could do. Windham married Agnes in August 1861, arranging a marriage settlement that gave her almost total control over his finances.

The couple went to Paris for their honeymoon, but Roberts reappeared as soon as they got back. The Windhams set off for Norfolk (by ECR, of course), with young Windham enjoying the ride on the locomotive footplate. Roberts spent the journey with Agnes, the guard reporting that they pulled down the blinds of their carriage and made a bed on which to celebrate their reunion. Windham was much more interested in driving the train.

The General brought the case in an attempt to prevent the family estates falling into the hands of Agnes and her lover, but the press portrayed him as a grasping and wicked old man. The case went against him when the sister of Mrs Llewellin alleged that the Llewellins and General Windham had plotted to deprive the young man of his inheritance. At the end of January 1862 the Jury interviewed young Windham privately. It took them only half an hour to reach their decision that he was 'of sound mind', presumably easing the fears of the nation's railway enthusiasts in doing so. General Windham was left to contemplate his share of the £150,000 legal costs, but young Windham also had to pay despite being the victor.

Windham travelled back to Norfolk in inimitable style – by ECR train, with a huge Union Jack dangling from the window. As if to scotch the allegations, Mrs Windham joined him at Felbrigg Hall. There he gave a dinner to all his tenants and, it was said, he began to contemplate a quieter life. However, that summer he was again spotted acting as a railway servant at

Figure 4.9 *Due perhaps to academic interest, a small crowd would often gather by the railway bridge at Cambridge to place bets on the arrival of trains in the early days of the ECR* Cambridgeshire Libraries

Cambridge and Ely! Travellers by ECR continued to fear that he might be driving their train.

The story has a sad ending. By June 1862 Windham had separated from his wife and had lost control of most of his property – much of it to Agnes. Though they enjoyed a brief period of reconciliation, as a result of which a child was born, the marriage never really functioned normally again. Young Windham took to driving his own coach around the Norfolk lanes, picking up passengers he happened to come across.

However, he was still active on the newly-formed GER in December 1862, for the Superintendent of the Line issued a warning to staff to prevent him from locking and unlocking carriages. Clearly Windham still had his friends though, for the warning also stated that any staff colluding with him would be sacked.

When Agnes secured control of the property in 1864 Windham was left penniless. He hung around the inns of Norwich until a coach proprietor named Bingham gave him a job driving the Norwich to Cromer coach for a guinea a week. Windham died in poverty and obscurity on 2 February 1866, but was buried in the family vault at Felbrigg.

5

Passengers' Tales

5.1 On and off the Trains

Especially in the early days, the railways of East Anglia were full of incidents which punctuated the supposedly smooth process of handling passengers. Sometimes the problems began even before the passengers could reach the station – at Ely the approach road was so bad in 1851 that it was commonly known as the 'Slough of Despond'.

Even today there are regular problems with passengers getting out of trains carelessly, but this was even more of a hazard when trains were a relative innovation. An incident of this type occurred at Brentwood in 1849, though it fortunately had a 'miraculous' conclusion. A passenger wishing to end his journey at Brentwood opened the carriage door and stepped out before the train had stopped properly. He lost his footing, slipped, and fell between platform edge and carriage. Staff rushed up, expecting to have to deal with a fatality, but discovered the passenger still alive beneath the carriage. He had fallen longitudinally between the rails; although his clothes were torn and the ticket in his pocket had been cut in two by the carriage wheel, the lucky traveller had received only slight arm injuries.

It would have been expected of senior officers of the Great Eastern to set a good example of safe behaviour. In 1892 James Shingler was Inspector of Trucks for the GER, but this did not stop him from behaving in a bizarre manner. Travelling on the 7 pm train from Liverpool Street, between Harold Wood and Brentwood Shingler suddenly stood up and opened the carriage door. To the astonishment of the others in the compartment, he then stepped out, falling heavily to the ground. Shingler was taken to the stationmaster's house at Harold Wood, but was found to have sustained nothing worse than a sprained ankle and some bruising. When asked why he had got out of a moving train, Shingler replied that he had 'gone far enough and wanted to go back.' He then went out and got a train back towards his home at Forest Gate.

Even more extraordinary than this was the behaviour of discharged soldier Thomas Langton in 1884. He was in a third-class carriage of a Liverpool Street to Ipswich train when the other passengers noticed that he had been drinking and was acting in a very agitated way. About 13 miles out of London he suddenly sprang up and leapt head first at the carriage window on the up side. That the window was shut made no difference to Langton, who shattered the glass and disappeared from view so quickly that other passengers had no time to do anything but make a despairing grab for his feet. When the train stopped at Colchester an emergency telegraph message was sent down the line. A rather dazed Langton was found on a piece of soft ground beside the line near Romford, the ground having recently been dug up. He had managed to leap from a down train completely across the up track and had landed in a garden! Langton told the Police that he had been in a compartment with two others who had started some 'foul play', so he had leapt out to escape from being robbed. This was denied by the other passengers, and Langton was taken to the local workhouse infirmary.

Sometimes these incidents had sadder conclusions. In 1854 an old man from Brundall went on a day trip to Great Yarmouth. When he returned to the station in the evening he found that there was no train to Brundall for some time, but that there was an excursion going back to Norwich that would make only

Figure 5.1 (*On facing page*) *Yarmouth Vauxhall Station in 1906, showing the Midland and Great Northern joint line passing to the west. Sidings extend beyond the station to the quays*
Ordnance Survey

62

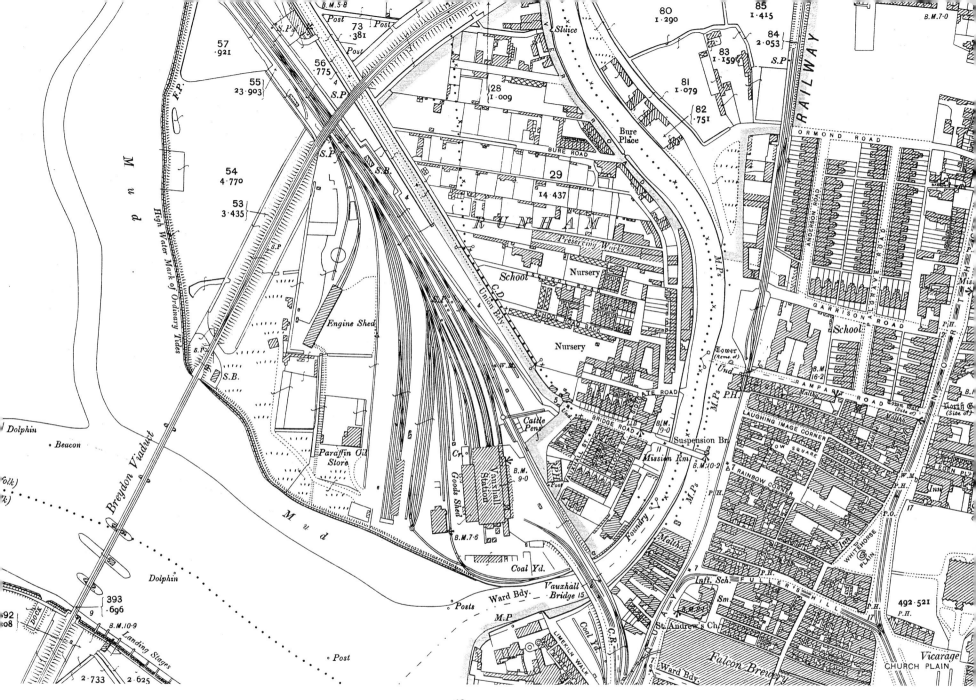

B.M.5.8

S.P.

Post 73 Post 381

Sluice

80 1.290

85 1.415

B.M.7.0

57 .921

S.P.

84 2.053

S.P.

Post

56 775

83 1.159

S.P.

55 23.903

S.P.

28 1.009

ORMOND ROAD

81 1.079

S.P.

Bure Place

82 .751

S.B.

54 4.770

Bure Road

ANDERSON ROAD

29 14.437

S.P.

53 3.435

R U N H A M

Preserving Works

School

Nursery

M.Ps

GARRISON ROAD

School

M u d

High Water Mark of Ordinary Tides

Engine Shed

Nursery

Tower (Rems. of)

B.M. 16.2

Und

C.D.

RAMPART ROAD

North G. (Site of)

S.P.

W.M.

Und

Dolphin

Beacon

Cattle Pens

Suspension Br.

LAUGHING IMAGE CORNER

Inn

W.M.

Paraffin Oil Store

TE ROAD

Mission Rm.

SQUARE

Eden Pl.

Breydon Viaduct

Cr.

Goods Shed

Vauxhall Station

B.M. 9.0

Post

BRIDGE ROAD

B.M.10.2

RAINBOW CORNER

Malth.

WHITEHORSE PLAIN

P.O.

olk)

B.M.7.6

Coal Yd.

Foundry

Malth.

FULLER'S HILL

P.H.

Dolphin

Ward Bdy.

Vauxhall Bridge 15

M u d

Posts

Inft. Sch.

Falcon Brewery

Vicarage

393 .696

M.P

Coal Yd.

St. Andrew's Ch.

CHURCH PLAIN

9

B.M.10.9

C.R.

492.521

P.H.

92 08

DOCK

Landing Stages

LIMEKILN WALK

Ward Bdy.

2.733 2.625

Post

63

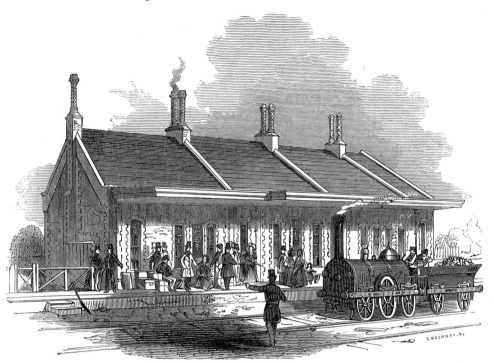

Figure 5.2   *Brandon Station at the time of opening in 1845*
Illustrated London News, 2 August 1845

one stop – at Reedham. The old man got on this train and travelled to Brundall, where he attempted to jump out as it ran through the station. He fell beneath the wheels and was killed, a victim of his own impatience.

Sad fatalities also occurred with passengers hurrying to catch trains as they were already pulling away from the station. An unusually prominent victim of this was the Conservative MP for Romford, James Theobald, who died from his injuries after such an incident at Romford station in March 1894. He attempted to board the 2.16 pm train to London after it had started and was crushed between the carriage footboard and the platform.

Some passengers were more cautious in their approach to rail travel. One such man was Thomas Porter of North End Farm, Felsted, near Braintree. Porter had never been on a train until his seventy-fifth birthday in January 1913. As a special treat he was taken for a return run from Felsted to Braintree, his view of the proceedings being recorded in *GERM*:

> The train went off very fast. I liked it all except the bridges. It seemed very dangerous to go under those small bridges so quick. I lay back and closed my eyes each time we got near to a bridge.

5.2   Matters Male and Female

As noted elsewhere, the railway's electric telegraph proved to be an important weapon in the fight against crime in Victorian England, but it also proved singularly successful in interrupting the course of true love, which had a tendency to develop into elopement.

One Friday evening in February 1847 a telegraph message was received at the ECR's Bishopsgate station. Transmitted from Ely, the message read:

> Detain a man in the three o'clock up train from Yarmouth. He is attired in a flannel jacket, fustian trousers and blue cap; has small whiskers and is accompanied by a female named Read. She is dressed in a dark gown and Tuscan bonnet, and has with her a child.

The couple were identified and detained by the station Police. Shortly afterwards another message arrived to explain the first; the man in the blue cap had 'run away with £30 and the prosecutor's wife'. The message advised that the enraged husband would arrive on the following train, but he did not. Nor could the missing £30 be found on the errant couple, so the Police released them. The next morning a Constable arrived from Whittlesea and was very annoyed to discover that they had been allowed to go.

Almost exactly two years later another telegraph message was received in London, this time requesting the detention of a young lady who was travelling from Cambridge. The young lady was found to have been travelling first class in the company of a gentleman. The young lady was given into the care of an uncle, leaving the 'disappointed swain in deep dejection'. The latter turned out to be a student, who had formed a relationship with the girl against her parents' wishes.

For a few years in mid-Victorian times, the press was full of stories about how dangerous it was for women to travel alone in the non-corridor compartment carriages then common. Problems were made worse on railways like the ECR which did not provide any carriage lights for night travel. One result of this was that Robert Ely of Norwich ended up in court in April 1851, charged with assaulting Mrs Hicks of Norwich.

Both Hicks and Ely were travelling in a Yarmouth to Norwich train in the evening and, typically, it was not lighted. About five minutes after they had started, Mrs Hicks felt a hand against her side and concluded that Ely was trying to steal from her basket.

She warned him off but a few minutes later felt his hand again; this time she told him to watch what he did with his hands. Ely was not dissuaded, but instead tried to kiss the alarmed woman. When she cried for help another young man in the compartment told her not to worry, as he would not hurt her. Mrs Hicks later gave evidence that Ely then 'put his hands over her person in an indecent manner.'

At Reedham another woman offered to help give Ely into custody, but the train was still in darkness. Ely still persisted and, according to the *Mercury*, 'behaved in a manner not fit to be stated in print.' Mrs Hicks fainted but help was at last available at Brundall, where the guard came to the rescue. Ely was found to be drunk and was handed over to the Police.

The question of providing lights in carriages rumbled on for

Figure 5.3   *A cutaway drawing of the carriage built for use on the GER for the Prince and Princess of Wales after their marriage in 1863. The couple would have been frequent users of the GER for visits to Sandringham and Newmarket*
Illustrated London News, 1863

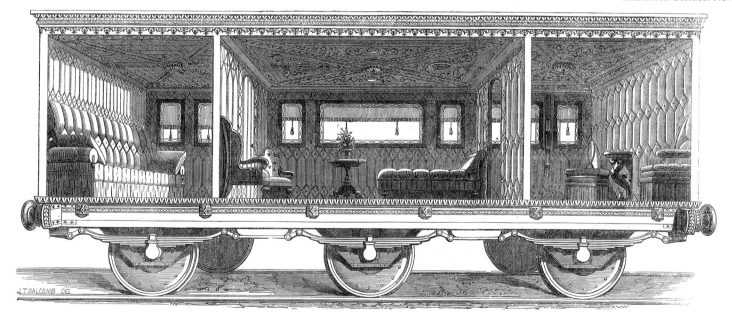

Figure 5.4 Chelmsford Station around 1910   Essex Record Office

several years. In October 1853 an annoyed passenger wrote to the *Cambridge Chronicle* to complain about the East Anglian Railway. Leaving Lynn in a second-class carriage of the 5.30 pm up train, he had requested lights but been refused. The same request was made at Downham Market, but again met with a negative response. The enraged passenger signed himself as 'A Traveller, and Protector of Female Travellers'. Victorian women simply could not venture onto a railway that put them in darkness with strange men.

However, if the *Braintree & Bocking Advertiser* of November 1859 is to be believed, it was not always the lone woman who was in danger from predatory members of the opposite sex. The following letter appeared under the heading 'Perils of Railway Travelling':

Some months ago I was seeking a second class carriage at the Shoreditch terminus. A pretty young lady attracted my notice by politely informing me that there was room in her compartment, politely pushing open the door at the same time. As soon as I was seated opposite to her she pulled to the door, as much as to say there was enough. We started, I very ungallantly engrossed in my newspaper, she silent, having no-one in the carriage but myself to speak to. I felt the carriage very narrow, and feared I was crowding her, and I moved back as far as I could. In a few moments I still felt her dress against me, and soon was really crowded, being pressed by her. Now, I confess with shame that, being a young man, I felt a little vanity at her attentions, and I yielded to temptation so far as not to move from her. In half an hour a gentleman got in, which, from the lady's face, was not an agreeable thing; she looked vexed. However, our silly conduct proceeded, she throughout taking the lead. At length the gentleman observed us, and my companion, blushing crimson at being discovered, very wickedly drew herself away from me, and flying to the opposite side said I had insulted her. When she found, moreover, that she was known to the thirdcomer, she became very indignant and screamed for the train to stop; that she had been grievously assaulted etc. I cannot tell you, sir, my confusion. I durst not charge her with being the first to commence – how cowardly it would have looked! – and upon reaching the terminus her brother was informed – not by the lady, but by the gentleman – how infamously I had insulted her. He flew at me like a tiger, thinking I had really ruined his sister; he smashed my new hat over my eyes, and being much bigger than myself, and assisted by the other passenger, gave me such an awful punishment, that I shall never forget it. They were then going to give me into custody; but on my appealing to her, she said that she would gladly have given me into the charge of the Police, but was too bashful to appear in a court of justice to prosecute; and so I got off.

Quite how much of this account was true it is now impossible to say, but it was clearly printed to amuse the Victorian readership and no doubt resulted in a large number of young men travelling hopefully along the Braintree branch!

Far more serious was the 1848 case in Colchester involving

Figure 5.5 *This postcard was used to depict many country lines – only the names ever changed!*
Essex Record Office

William Douglas, a porter at the town's railway station. One evening that year Agnes Lewin, a young servant woman, arrived at the station on her own and could not find a cab to take her home. Douglas, who had clearly been watching for such an opportunity, offered to help her find a cab by escorting her to the Waggon & Horses public house. At the pub, Douglas engaged a cab driven by James Keys and Agnes Lewin climbed into it. She was horrified when Douglas followed her inside; he then proceeded to commit a brutal and callous assault in which Keys must have been a conspirator. The poor woman 'called out and resisted to the utmost of her powers; but afterwards became insensible.' Douglas was punished with two years hard labour and was presumably sacked by the ECR.

Figure 5.6 *Ely Station in about 1905*   Cambridgeshire Libraries

5.3 Passengers and the Courts

In the late 1840s and early 1850s, the ECR and the other East Anglian railways gained a bad reputation for their treatment of passengers. The lack of lights in the trains was one part of this, but a case brought before Shoreditch County Court in April 1850 involved the absorbing topic of wet seats. A Mr Frost brought an action against the ECR for the recovery of 1s 6d, which he had been forced to spend as the third-class seats in his train had been too wet; he had thus gone first class. The Judge, clearly familiar with the ECR, expressed sympathy for Frost but the ECR was able to prove that he had been offered an alternative third-class seat that was dry. Thus he lost the case.

There were many cases brought by passengers who wanted damages for injuries sustained during their journeys. An unusual one was the February 1851 case of Farrell (Pauper) v.

ECR. Mrs Farrell was a costermonger, making her living from selling fruit in the streets – a far from lucrative profession. On 22 June 1850 she was returning to London by train and, in getting out at Shoreditch, slipped and fell. She slid down between platform edge and carriage, where she remained for 15 minutes before anyone could extract her. The accident resulted in a broken thigh and injured back, putting Mrs Farrell out of work so that she was forced to go on the Poor Law. It was the Poor Law authorities who brought the case against the ECR.

At the hearing it was alleged that she had fallen because the train had started moving again after it had stopped. However, the ECR had prepared a solid defence; the surgeon who had attended Mrs Farrell at the hospital said that she had smelt strongly of spirits, whilst the nurse who had undressed her reported finding two bladders of spirits on her. Not surprisingly, the court found for the ECR.

Another passenger who had a difficult journey was a Mr Thompson. On 11 November 1851 Thompson arrived at Ilford station and bought a third-class ticket for London. He intended to catch a Colchester to London train, but this was running ten minutes late. When it reached Ilford the guard was rushing about trying to catch up the lost time; he was, as the *Essex Standard* reported, 'off his guard'. Because of this Thompson was directed by mistake into a second-class carriage.

At Stratford Thompson was stopped by a ticket inspector, who demanded the 5d difference between third and second-class fares. Thompson only had 2½d on him, so he was taken into custody and kept at the Police station overnight. The next day he was brought before the Magistrates and fined 2s 6d plus costs; to pay this and ensure his release from custody, Thompson had to pawn his watch.

He was rather aggrieved about all this and brought a case against the ECR for wrongful imprisonment and assault, claiming £50 damages. He won the case, but was awarded only £25 12s damages.

'Breach of contract' cases also emerged on occasions. In March

Figure 5.7   *A busy scene at Brentwood in August 1908 as T19 Class No. 1036 leads the 10.10 am Yarmouth to Liverpool Street down from Ingrave, overtaking the 2.50 am goods from Ipswich behind Y14 No. 915*   LCGB K. Nunn Coll.

1853 the ECR was sued by a Mr Fox for breach of contract. Fox brought his case as a result of a dreadful experience in trying to travel from London to Bures, in Suffolk, on Christmas Day 1852. The train was two hours late leaving London and Fox missed his connection at Marks Tey as a result. He thus hired a horse and cart to take him to Bures and claimed the cost of this from the ECR.

The ECR defended itself by reporting the extraordinarily large number of passengers who had been dealt with at Bishopsgate station on Christmas morning. Over 1,500 people had been despatched into the country, with trains to Colchester leaving at 7.50, 8.45, and 9.30 am. Another extra train had been arranged for Marks Tey and the Sudbury line passengers, but the ECR claimed that Fox had refused to wait for this and was thus himself to blame for the lack of a train to Bures when he arrived at Marks Tey. The case against the ECR was dismissed.

Most railways received many claims for injury, some being amazingly minor. One such was the 'Bad Knee Case' of July 1862. This involved a five-year-old boy who had been travelling from Lea Bridge to Bishopsgate in the company of his mother and sister. However the journey was rudely interrupted when the train ran into a line of trucks; the boy was jolted off his mother's lap, and fell to the floor, injuring his knee. According to the mother's evidence, the boy at first cried and limped, but eventually his leg became 'contracted' and 'imperfect.' In its defence, the ECR pointed out that it took several months for the mother to bring her case forward, and the claim for compensation was rejected.

The railway companies were always anxious to avoid lengthy legal battles. On 9 October 1860 a man fell when alighting at Woodford and sued the Railway as a result. On 13 February 1861 a similar accident occurred at the same station and for a second time stationmaster Taylor failed to report it. As the first passenger had won his case, the Board sacked Taylor for neglecting his duties and so exposing them to bad publicity and legal action.

So many people tried to extract money out of railways by devious legal actions that they began to be viewed as dubious, to the benefit of the railways. The GER gained another successful result in the 1871 case of Gill v. GER. Gill had been a passenger in the rear carriage of a train and when the train stopped at a station it was not fully drawn up. Gill had to get out without the benefit of the platform lights and, as a result, claimed that he was injured. The GER was able to prove that he had jumped out of the train, whereas other passengers had climbed out carefully.

A most unusual case was heard in the Norfolk courts in July 1890, attracting great interest as the man in trouble was the deputy Lord Lieutenant of the county, Algernon C. Fountaine

of Narford Hall, Swaffham, charged with stopping a GER express train at East Winch on 18 March 1890. Fountaine had gone to the station in a hurry and had tried to get the stationmaster to arrange for the next express train to make an unscheduled stop to pick him up. Unmoved by the high social position of the intending passenger, the stationmaster stuck to the rules and refused. Fountaine decided to take matters into his own hands and, as the express approached, leapt onto the track and started waving his arms about. Miraculously the train managed to stop in time, but Fountaine was arrested and in the end was fined £25.

5.4   The Problems of Being a Passenger

Although a great deal has been claimed for the punctuality of the later GER 'Jazz Service', the fact is that the GER inherited a poor reputation and had to work hard to win itself a better name under energetic managers like Parkes, who became known as 'Punctuality Parkes'. In 1904 G. P. Neale wrote that, 'to the surprise of most railway men', the GER was the most

Figure 5.8   *The 11.20 am to Hunstanton leaves King's Lynn on 13 September 1910 behind T19 No. 759*   LCGB K. Nunn Coll.

punctual of the southern railways, whilst in 1918 E. L. Ahrons commented that the GER was 'a most punctual line in spite of many difficulties in London.'

The experience of the passengers, though, was sometimes far from amusing. Rev. G. Barrett was so enraged after he made a journey on the GER in 1874 that he wrote a long letter to *The Times*, which published it in full. Barrett had wanted to go from Norwich to Beccles on a Saturday evening in December. He checked the schedules and found that he could leave Norwich at 7.45 pm, change at Tivetshall, then take a branch train along the Waveney Valley line to arrive at Beccles at 9.28 pm. In the event, his schedule proved to be rather different: he reached Tivetshall at 8.20 pm, did not leave it until 1.07 am and finally arrived at Beccles at 2.20 am on Sunday!

The background to this tale reveals a sad lack of management

Figure 5.9   *C53 tram engine No. 130 shunting wagons at Ipswich quay in April 1910*   LCGB K. Nunn Coll.

skills among the more rural GER staff. The main-line train from Norwich reached Tivetshall more or less on time; there it was meant to connect with a train from Beccles and take its passengers on to Diss and the south, whilst the Beccles train would then return along the Waveney Valley with the passengers who had arrived from Norwich. However, there was no sign at Tivetshall of any train from Beccles, and while the main-line train waited for the connecting service a grim tale developed.

At about 6 pm a train had broken down on the single-line branch at Harleston. Since the branch was worked on the staff system, the breakdown train could not proceed from Beccles until someone had collected the staff off the failed train. Some of the crew from the 'delinquent engine' were therefore despatched by road to Beccles with the staff. The breakdown train then set out for Harleston, collected the errant locomotive, and returned with everything to Beccles. Only after things had been sorted out at Beccles did anyone think about running a train up to Tivetshall.

Meanwhile back at the junction, passengers were feeling miserable. The *Norwich Mercury* explained their plight with some sympathy: 'Those who have been unhappy enough ever to stop at Tivetshall will know what kind of a place it is to be detained in for five hours on one of the most inclement nights we have had this year.'

Rev. Barrett was thoroughly frozen by this time. At 11 pm the main-line train suddenly despaired of making any connection and set off southwards into the darkness; having waited 2 hrs 40 mins, it managed to leave without the correct signal clearance and with the guard and some of the passengers left behind on the station!

But all hope was not lost. Rev. Barrett wrote that '. . . at 11.27 pm our ears at Tivetshall were gladdened by the sound of the long-expected train coming in.' Many of those who wished to go to Beccles immediately clambered on board, leaving those who had arrived from Beccles and wanted to go to Diss wondering what to do. Barrett found himself a snug corner in a carriage and was dozing happily when he was disturbed by a sudden influx of cattlemen and farmers. Then he was told to get out again, having gone nowhere.

It had been decided to run the Beccles train forward to Diss so as to deliver the passengers who had missed the main-line train. So Barrett had to wait another hour until the train got back from Diss. Thus a journey from Norwich to Beccles occupied six hours of the clergyman's life. He only had one solution to the problem: the Midland Railway should immediately build a line into Norfolk.

A story in the *GERM* in 1912 described a time when the ECR was known as the 'pariah of railways'. At about the period 1856–7, the magazine claimed, it took 1 hr 45 mins to travel from Fenchurch Street to Custom House. This clearly had an effect on the sanity of the passengers, for one official reported making the journey in the same compartment as a strange Irishman. The latter spent the whole of the journey muttering, 'Blackguard Eastern Counties! Old iron and firewood! Blackguard Eastern Counties!' One can only assume that the phrase 'old iron and firewood' referred to the style of construction of an ECR train.

Conditions for winter travel were extremely primitive in the early days. Reference is made elsewhere to the problems caused by a lack of carriage lights, but of course there was also no carriage heating. Passengers could expect to find better facilities at the stations, but this was not always so. A letter to the *Cambridge Chronicle* in January 1850 complained of a lack of heating at Whittlesea station. For once the blame could not be laid at the door of a cost-conscious ECR, for there were at least three stoves provided for the benefit of passengers. The only problem was that there was 'not a glimmer in one of them, except that appropriated for the comfort of the Clerk's person which is supposed to be the seat of honour.'

For the third-class and 'Parliamentary' trains, the ECR provided carriages with 'louvre boarding' rather than glazed windows and ventilators. In August 1857 the Board of Trade hinted that they might not approve the ECR's timetables for Parliamentary trains unless proper windows were installed, thus render-

ing the ECR open to an expensive penalty. Sinclair, who was responsible for ECR carriages, was surprised by this new tactic and advised the Board to do nothing about it. The Board of Trade did not push the issue, and so the poor passengers continued to enjoy draughty travelling on the ECR, consoled (if anyone thought to tell them) that new carriages were better-designed while the old ones were being modified as they went through the repair shops.

An extremely emotive issue in the early days of the ECR was that of smoking in the trains. The ECR was the first railway in the country to provide carriages for smokers, in 1846. In 1854 the directors ordered the provision of a smoking carriage for each class on each train, but smokers still persisted in lighting up in whichever carriage they happened to find themselves in. In January 1856 the *Cambridge Chronicle* called for tougher penalties for smokers on trains. These villainous people were described as 'Thoughtless young men or callous brutes who care for nothing but their own gratification.'

However these 'callous brutes' sometimes brought heavy penalties upon themselves. In 1874 George Rands, an Ipswich sack manufacturer, was charged with 'interfering with the comfort of the passengers in a railway carriage' at Haughley on 18 September 1873. Rands had been travelling between Diss and Finningham when he had lit a match with the clear intention of smoking. Another male passenger warned Rands not to smoke since the carriage was not a 'smoker', but Rands claimed that it *was* a smoker. He also called the other passenger 'a damned humbug'. At Finningham the other passenger changed carriages, and then at Haughley told the guard about Rands's behaviour. As a result of this the guard, Charles Death, and the passenger, Swanston, were witnesses in the case against Rands.

The trial proved to be a very bad-tempered affair. Rands defended himself by claiming that he had been misled by a GER man at Finningham who had assured him that the carriage was a smoker. But there were also rumours and counter-rumours about the characters of the defendant and the key

Workman (politely, to old lady, who has accidentally got into a smoking compartment). "You don't object to my pipe, I 'ope, mum?"
Old Lady. "Yes, I *do* object, very strongly!"
Workman. "Oh! Then out you get!!"

Figure 5.10   Punch *cartoon from the 1870s*

witness, Swanston. 'Fraudulent bankruptcy' was muttered about in connection with Rands, whilst Swanston also alleged that Rands would have 'led astray' two young ladies in the

carriage had it not been for the intervention of the guard. Rands counter-claimed by saying that Swanston was a typical tee-totaller – always interfering and making comments. Rands lost the case however and was fined 20s with 16s 6d costs.

The allowing of smoking at all in trains was a very liberal gesture compared to how things had first been on the railways. One of the first bye-laws of the ECR had banned smoking completely; on one occasion a guard was rumoured to have snatched a cigar out of the surprised mouth of a transgressing first-class passenger!

Rands's offences were minor compared to those of William Collison, a passenger from Durham who incurred the wrath of the GER at Christmas 1873. Although Collison was 'a respectable looking man', his list of offences was quite impressive. He was charged by the GER with:

> . . . being drunk whilst in one of their carriages, refusing to give up his ticket when requested to do so, assaulting one of their officers whilst in the execution of their duty, with using abusive language to one of their Inspectors, and creating a nuisance on their station platform.

Collison was on his way to King's Lynn for Christmas when the troubles started. He took the 7.35 pm from Ely and was already the worse for drink when he got on it. The ticket collector on the train had difficulty with Collison as he refused to show his ticket. Inspector Bigg and two staff at King's Lynn got the drunken man out of the train and onto the platform, taking out his bag as well. Collison did not like this treatment and followed Bigg to the parcels office where he abused the Inspector and spat in his face.

At the trial before the Mayor of Lynn, Collison protested that he could not remember anything about the events – the usual excuse of the drunkard. He argued that he was not the sort of person who did that sort of thing: 'I am quite harmless, and as for using the bad words, I never use bad words . . . '

The Mayor found Collison guilty but fined him the nominal sum of 1s, then launched an attack on the GER. The act of removing Collison's bag from the train seems to have infuriated the Mayor's typically Victorian sense of the sanctity of property: 'They might as well take [a passenger's] coat from their back, or the collar off their necks', he moaned.

5.5   A Long, Long Day Trip to Wells

The independent days of the ECR were already numbered when, in September 1861, the Norfolk press was forced into even stronger condemnation than usual. The Directors of the Eastern Counties and Norfolk railways were labelled 'delinquents' and, it was said, deserved 'the strongest censure that could be heaped upon them.' Fortunately this outburst of anger

provides us with a delightful view today of how life must have been on a mid-Victorian branch line.

The comments above were only a small part of a barrage of abuse. The two Railways had created chaos for thousands and, it was said, turned the normally peaceful towns of Wells and Yarmouth into the equivalent of the Wild West, with men firing off weapons in all directions to the terror of ladies.

The cause of all the trouble was the review of the Norfolk Volunteers (the equivalent of today's Territorials) at Wells. This involved moving several thousand men, from all over the county, to Wells; numerous special trains were required, but

Figure 5.11   *Cromer Station in the 1880s*   Norwich Library

there was only a single line to handle the traffic between Dereham and Wells. It was a task to which the joint efforts of the two railways were eminently unsuited!

Problems started even before there were any trains running. Sensing a financial bonanza, the ECR refused to negotiate any reduced terms for moving all the Volunteers, contrary to practice on most other railways in the kingdom. Despite this, the ECR and the Norfolk Railway were engaged by the authorities to ferry several thousand men to Wells and back within set time limits – which, as the day unfolded, proved hopelessly unrealistic for these two companies.

Some of the excursions were due to leave Yarmouth at 6 am and Norwich at 7 am, scheduled to reach Wells by 10 am. Since it was only 43 miles from Norwich to Wells, this hardly demanded exhaustive running.

Trouble began before the Norwich contingent had started their journey. The Corps met at the Shire Hall just as dawn was breaking, and marched to Thorpe station in good time for the 7 am departure. However, a very long time elapsed between the entrainment of the soldiers and the departure of the train! A Norwich rifleman sent in his account of the journey to the local newspaper, complaining that the time spent at Thorpe was excruciatingly boring. The Corps band were all in one carriage so they were able to amuse themselves by playing a few tunes, but the other Volunteers had to pass the time by sending ECR employees off on bogus errands.

Eventually the train jerked into a sort of motion and set off at a modest pace for Wymondham, where it turned onto the branch-line as far as Dereham. At Dereham it stopped – and remained stopped for a very long time. As the delay stretched to over two hours the soldiers started to get restless once more, some even directing the harassed Dereham stationmaster to lend a hand by pushing their train. Others asked him if it was possible to rent a bed for the night.

As they were carrying ammunition, the Volunteers were not allowed to smoke in the train. A large number therefore clambered out onto the platform, but various jokers took to yelling 'Fall in!' in officer-like tones, so that the Volunteers would leap back into the carriages in the false belief that the long wait was over. The principal beneficiary of the delay was the proprietor of the station refreshment rooms, who did a roaring trade. Meanwhile, a queue of five other trains had built up behind the Norwich Corps's excursion.

Eventually the cause of the delay was revealed. Something had gone wrong with the system of working the single line between Dereham and Fakenham; this was variously reported as being a fault with the telegraph or that the single-line token had been lost! A train from Wells had stopped at Fakenham, and neither it nor the Volunteers' excursion could proceed until the problem was sorted out.

After a delay of over two hours the train from Wells drew into Dereham station, clearing the line for the Norwich Corps to proceed. It was noted that the train from Fakenham, which had kept six packed trains waiting, contained less than two dozen passengers. The *Norwich Mercury*'s reporter was forced to observe that 'even a delay at an Eastern Counties station will have a termination' (not mentioning that he had borrowed the phrase), but even so 'it was the dreariest two hours I have ever spent.'

The trains then trundled forwards to Wells, where the Norwich Corps were given some beer in a field by the station before being marched off to the review. From getting into the train at Thorpe to getting out again at Wells, their journey had occupied over six hours!

The events of the day were disrupted badly, but the agonies did not conclude there as the railways proved equally inept at getting the men home again. Most of the soldiers returned to the field by the station shortly after 7 pm, with the first trains for Norwich arranged to leave just after 8 pm. This timetable proved to be highly fictitious.

8 pm came and went with no sign of a train. Boredom again became a problem, especially as some of the Volunteers had been drinking excessively. Fed up with waiting at the station, they began to roam the streets looking for amusement. It was

reported that some started firing their carbines as road vehicles passed, and that others let off their guns to frighten young ladies. One man complained of their behaviour but was 'greeted with a volley of the coarsest and vilest expressions.' Mysteriously, no one could locate the officers!

At about 11 pm a train finally arrived at the station, ready to take the Volunteers back to Norwich. However a huge number of people, including many members of the public, were now waiting at the station and they scrambled into the train before the Volunteers, 'some going head first through the windows of the unlocked doors', such was their desperation to get home.

The Volunteer officers, who arrived next, protested about the invasion of their special train, but ECR staff made only a token effort to restore the rightful arrangements – a single young lady was pulled out before the train started. To add insult to injury, thirsty Volunteers were charged 1d per pint of water from the railway cisterns at Wells and Dereham.

A second train departed from Wells at half past midnight, and returning Volunteers gave 'three groans' for the ECR at Thorpe station. It was 4.20 am before the Norwich men reached their home city.

In all the confusion, nineteen of the Yarmouth Volunteers got left behind, probably because they had been drinking too much. By all accounts the drink added further stresses to the homeward journey as several soldiers were ill in the crowded trains.

The ECR deposited the Yarmouth men back home in the early hours of the morning. A number of them made matters worse by rampaging around the town firing their cannons, frightening the sleepy citizens.

It was generally agreed that the experience of the Wells Volunteers' Review formed a notably black day in the history of

Figure 5.12 *Sharp Stewart 2–4–0 No. 33 arrives at Wymondham off the Wells line with the 7.13 am Wells to Norwich on 6 April 1910*   LCGB K. Nunn Coll.

the ECR. The *Norwich Mercury* concluded: 'It is often said that Companies, and particularly the Eastern Counties Company, are dead to the honourable feelings which ought to regulate the management and conduct of a public company.' How true this was of the ECR!

6

Legal Affairs

Railways have always attracted the attention of the idle or the curious, and the ECR and the GER suffered as much in this respect as BR does today.

A combination of curiosity and ignorance proved an especial problem in the early days of railways. So it was that Josiah Thorogood was charged in December 1840 with 'setting in motion a railway engine' as a result of which life was endang-

ered. Thorogood was something of an early train-spotter and was in the habit of hanging around the construction depot at Shenfield, where he decided to take a closer look at a locomotive that had been left in steam while its crew had their supper. Thorogood was fairly drunk, but he none the less managed to clamber onto the footplate and set the loco into motion with a jerk.

As it lurched forwards Thorogood fell off the footplate, but the engine continued on its way down the line. It knocked a carriage off the track but fortunately the line was incomplete and it soon ran out of track. It was lucky that the engine had headed out into the country, for if it had set off towards London a serious accident could have resulted. Thorogood was fined £5 and given six months in prison.

A clearly more deliberate and callous act occurred at Littlebury in 1860, following which a man was given twelve months' hard labour. He had 'altered a signal', with apparent intent to endanger life.

Petty acts of vandalism occurred all the time, the method of punishment usually being of the 'short, sharp shock' variety. To take one example, two Copford schoolboys spent a day in 1899 putting stones on the line near Colchester. The driver of an up train found 41 stones on one rail – over which the continental express was expected at any moment. When apprehended, the schoolboys each blamed the other (true schoolboy style); one received twelve strokes of the birch, the other six.

The railways were also frequent victims of robberies, though the GER did not suffer as spectacularly as the South Eastern or Great Western did. Perhaps the robbers believed that nothing

Figure 6.1 One of the two tunnels at Littlebury. The Arms are those of Lord Braybrooke, owner of Audley End House and a keen supporter of the Cambridge Line
Illustrated London News, 2 August 1845

of any great value could possibly be entrusted to the ECR or GER.

Country stations and goods trains in sidings were the favorite targets. At Histon station, near Cambridge, three sacks of potatoes and two sacks of wheat were stolen in 1850. Three local men were arrested. It was a typically opportunist crime with goods being removed that were lying conveniently to hand.

A similar case resulted in two men being put on trial in January 1856 for stealing grain from 'Ickleton' station (presumably Whittlesford). It was alleged that on the evening the grain disappeared they had been seen dragging corn from the direction of the station, some of which spilled in the road. However the sacks were not found in the possession of the prisoners, only nearby, and there were doubts over identification. They were acquitted.

In August 1881 there was a burglary at Cambridge station which aroused suspicions of an 'inside job'. Thieves broke into the GER booking office and stole £5 in cash, but they failed to get into the safe which contained hundreds of pounds. They also attempted to raid the Midland Railway's office at the same station. The station's Inspector of Police was questioned closely since the thieves seemed to know the habits of the station staff; the burglaries appeared to have been committed while the night staff were having their supper. No one was caught.

Most thefts of railway property or goods traffic were committed by railway employees and so are dealt with in the section on staff in Chapter 4. But the railway traveller had another hazard to face – pickpockets.

Pickpockets often worked in groups so that the 'tooler' (who actually made the 'lift') could pass the stolen property on to accomplices and thus avoid being caught with the evidence. This made it necessary to operate in crowded places where a good deal of honest jostling would be going on. Crowded railway stations were ideal haunts for such thieves.

In December 1852 Mrs Newton was caught up in heavy pre-Christmas traffic at Ely. As she was getting into the Cambridge train she was pushed and shoved from behind by strangers. Only as the train was leaving the station did she discover that £7 was missing from her pockets. By this time the culprits had made a rapid escape.

A Norwich gang made a regular habit of picking pockets at stations in 1852–3. At Ipswich station in September 1853 the stationmaster had been alerted by several complaints of theft during the day, and became suspicious of a woman later identified as Elizabeth Warren. A porter was instructed to keep a close watch and saw Warren go onto the platform where she

Figure 6.2 'Ickleton' Station, south of Cambridge. No record of a station of that name has been found, and probably it was in fact Whittlesford Station
Illustrated London News, 2 August 1845

Figure 6.3 *Norwich Victoria Station, the EUR terminus. The small station was largely superseded by Thorpe in the 1880s, but continued in operation until 1916*

Norwich Libraries

'hustled' a lady's dress. This was a way of 'fanning' the cloth to reveal a bulky object, such as a purse, if it was in the pocket.

The passenger looked down to discover that her handkerchief was half out of her pocket and her purse had gone. Warren was arrested by the railway staff but went down on her knees to plead that she was innocent. It was discovered that she had already been in Norwich gaol for similar offences, as had her lover; indeed the gaol chaplain had conducted a marriage service and paid the licence fees for them during their last stay at the gaol. It wasn't long before Warren was back there.

Norwich thieves were again arrested at Yarmouth in 1854. They had gone there to mingle with the crowds at the station very late in the evening. One person was caught robbing an old lady of a gold watch and sentenced to three months in prison.

Habitual criminals like these would have found the railways very useful since they could 'work' in places where their faces were less likely to be recognised by the authorities. Only a stupid Norwich thief would have considered operating at Norwich station after he had had an arrest or two.

Special events that attracted large crowds were useful to pickpockets. The Harwich Naval Review of 1863 attracted such large crowds that pickpockets were at work long before most people actually got to Harwich. Philip Bennet was among the throngs of passengers waiting at Witham station for a train to Harwich when he felt a man brush against him. He looked down and found that his purse had been half-lifted out of his pocket. Bennet pursued the suspicious man into the station lavatory and, with the aid of a porter, trapped him there. Bennet then found that he had lost his watch, which had been removed from its chain. James MacDonald, imprisoned in the toilet, was not to blame for this; his accomplice, Joseph Smith, was. Both men were said to be members of the London 'swell mob' and were each given three months hard labour.

Figure 6.4   Norwich Victoria Station in about 1900, showing the cramped position of the former EUR terminus   Ordnance Survey

In sad contrast was the situation of Daniel Price, described as 'a miserable-looking being.' Price was destitute and a regular visitor to the workhouse. A Constable saw him acting suspiciously in the GER's yard at Harwich and, keeping a close watch, saw Price steal 28 lb. of coal from the GER's stockpile. For this the poor man was given 31 days' hard labour.

As will have been seen from the section on prize-fight specials in Chapter 3, the ECR did not have a good reputation for encouraging law and order. However, the authorities soon realised that railways in general offered an effective way of handling the occasional outbreaks of mass violence that occurred throughout the country. Troops could be summoned by telegraph and then moved rapidly from place to place by railway.

The Norfolk Railway between Norwich and Yarmouth, opened in 1844, played a key role in the Yarmouth Riots of 22 February 1851. At this time the Norfolk Railway was independent, but for all practical purposes it was a part of the ECR which operated all the services before finally absorbing it in 1854. The Yarmouth Riots started with a dispute over wages between the shipowners and the fishermen. There had been a strike and tempers among the sailors were running high, especially as some men were being compelled to go back to work by law. One Yarmouth man was brought to court in order to be escorted by police to his ship, but a crowd of seamen attacked the police. About a dozen rioters were arrested and the individual at the centre of the row was put on board a tug bound for Lowestoft.

The arrested rioters were taken to Yarmouth Police station where a huge crowd of over 2,000 people gathered to rescue them. A ship's mast was used as a battering ram to break in and liberate the prisoners. The Police station was defended by 20 officers, plus a few men from the Militia and some Revenue officers. The Riot Act was read out and a hundred 'specials' sworn in. A desperate telegraph message was sent to Norwich, summoning help from the 11th Hussars; this was sent on the Railway's apparatus.

The message reached Norwich at 4.30 pm. Martin, the Norfolk Railway's Superintendent, made such hasty arrangements that the first troop train was approaching Yarmouth by 6.15 pm with another one following a short way behind.

The mob soon discovered what was happening and assembled at the station where they threatened to pull up the rails to keep the troop trains out, and to disconnect the telegraph. The Mayor was sent for and he authorised Captain Douglas of the Hussars to quell the riot at the station, which he did. The military then cleared the streets of the town, sending troublemakers scurrying for shelter.

The railways were not shown in such good light by the extraordinary proceedings during the construction of the Mistley, Thorpe & Walton Railway in Essex. The MTWR's lack of money was matched only by its contractor's difficulties, and early in 1866 it was decided that contractor Munro should give up the work and let another contractor complete it. At first the arrangement seemed satisfactory, but then a number of disputes arose over payments for work done and materials used. Munro refused to give up possession of what he had already built, and the MTWR decided to remove him and his navvies by force.

The operation was conducted in such a way as to suggest that the MTWR officers were men of frustrated military ambitions. Various of them were satirised in the local press as 'Engineer-General Cooke' and 'Secretary General Size', whilst the 'defence' was led by 'General Fryer'. Fryer was Munro's agent, and had a force of about 50 navvies at his disposal; the Railway recruited about 60 longshoremen from the Harwich district.

The initiative was grabbed by Fryer who stationed his men at the head of the cutting where they could not be attacked from the rear or outflanked. Eventually a frontal assault by the Harwich men resulted in the capture of Fryer, who was removed from the Railway's property. Fryer was not fainthearted, and he regrouped with his men at the head of another cutting nearby. He was removed swiftly this time, and when he attempted to make a third stand the navvies seemed to give up the struggle.

Perhaps it was Munro and Fryer who had the last laugh in the affair though. 1866 was not a good year for railway promotion since there were a number of financial disasters in the City; given this climate, the MTWR was never able to complete its line. A few overgrown cuttings are all that are left to show for the hard-won battle at Bradfield, near Mistley.

Legal problems also arose in trespass cases. Near Lowestoft the public insisted on walking along the railway to Mutford Bridge as it was shorter than going by road. The legal situation was complex as the railway followed an ancient right of way and the Company should have provided a fenced-off path. Results were tragic, since George Cook was killed by a Norwich to Lowestoft train near Mutford station in January 1861.

More extraordinary was the question of locomotives committing trespass. One or two early railway Companies allowed private traders to run their own trains over Company lines, and the law in this area was very uncertain. The practice was rare in non-industrial areas, so the ECR must have been surprised to receive a letter from coal merchant Henry Hunt in September 1857. Hunt wrote to ask that the ECR's engineer would:

> inspect one of my locomotive engines now in the engine works of the North London Railway Company at Bow which engine it is my intention to make use of for working my coals from the Blackwall Wharf to my various depots on your lines. And I wish you to take notice that I make this application in accordance with the clause 201 of the 6&7Wm. 4th cap. 106 [the original ECR Act of Parliament] – the above-mentioned engine is marked no. 2. I also give you notice that I shall require a like inspection of a second engine intended to be used in a like manner and marked no. 1 which said engine will be ready for inspection at the same place on Saturday, 19 September, 1857.

The ECR Board instructed its engineer, Sinclair, to inspect the engines in keeping with their own Act of Parliament which stated that other people's locomotives could be used if approved and certificated by the ECR. The Company had to have engines inspected and reported on within 14 days of being given notice, provided that they were within five miles of the ECR. A fine

Figure 6.5   *Class G15 No. 132 on the train from Upwell, approaching Wisbech in July 1912. Note the enclosed motion, which the GER was legally obliged to provide on this line*   LCGB K. Nunn Coll.

of up to £20 was fixed for using an engine without a certificate or after notice had been given to remove or stop using an unsatisfactory one. The ECR was also authorised to remove any offending engine from the railway.

When the ECR Board met on 15 October 1857 they heard that Hunt, his driver, and his stoker had been summonsed and the case was being heard at Worship Street court. It would seem that Hunt had used his locomotive without it having successfully obtained the necessary certificate. The Board had just resolved that their Traffic Committee should 'consider proper regulations' when ECR Superintendent Robertson arrived

Figure 6.6   *Hook of Holland Express. P43 Class 4–2–2 leaving the south end of Ipswich tunnel in about 1905*   Author's coll:

hot-foot from Worship Street. He carried the news that Hunt had been fined £5 plus costs, following which the charges against the driver and stoker had been withdrawn.

Possibly the ECR Board thought that this sorted out the Hunt problem, but the coal merchant would not accept defeat. On 29 October, when the ECR solicitors made a full report (revealing that costs were £12 9s 6d), the Board was also told that Hunt had written to say that he intended to proceed against the ECR for recovery of the money he had had to pay over, and for damages and losses arising from the illegal seizure and detention of his locomotive. It must have been the only occasion

when an engine was the victim in a case of 'wrongful arrest'. To add further insult, Hunt repeated his request for a certificate, and asked for a book of regulations for his driver's use.

The Board decided that an extensive, privately-hauled coal traffic would be a danger to the public and that they would continue to refuse a certificate. They also decided to write to other railway companies with the object of pressuring the Board of Trade into curtailing what they saw as a dangerous practice.

And who was the determined Mr Hunt? It seems likely that he was an agent, or even a partner, in the Northumberland & Durham Coal Company. This firm seems to have acted as a wholesaler and distributor in the London area and was not an owner of northern coalmines. Coal sidings on the North London Railway at Hackney, Kingsland, and Islington were taken over by the Company on 20 October 1851. From about that date they worked coal trains with their own engines and men from Poplar Docks to these sidings, to which others were later added, with coal drops at places where the railway was above the street. The Coal Company was allowed to operate its trains at night only, for a number of years, although there is evidence to suggest that the NLR occasionally found the practice to be a risky one.

The Coal Company owned five locomotives, all built by Robert Stephenson & Co., of which four were delivered in 1851. The NLR took over the working of the coal trains on 20 January 1858; it purchased the five engines, the wagons, and some plant for £43,000.

It would seem that Hunt's campaign against the ECR was prompted by a change in the Coal Company's relationship with its other host, the NLR. Perhaps he wanted to find fresh markets which could be served by his locomotives and trucks, which were themselves a costly investment. His problem appears to have been solved by the purchase of the equipment by the NLR, at what seems to have been a very generous price; perhaps Hunt's argument with the ECR was his way of getting the NLR to worry about potential lost traffic.

Like many big businesses, the ECR and GER were often

Figure 6.7 *Cromer Station (GER), later Cromer High, at about the time of its opening in 1877*   Norwich Library

involved in legal cases where negligence was alleged. In 1871 the GER was sued for £18 10s following the loss of a haystack and twelve yards of hedgerow in July 1870. This common occurrence was of course due to sparks from an engine. A train passing through Loughton had caused the damage, though GER platelayers helped to put the fire out. Later the same day there was another fire. The GER was found to be not guilty as there was no evidence of negligence; no doubt other railways breathed a sigh of relief at the outcome of the case.

A similar case had occurred in 1861 when the ECR was taken to court by a man whose son had been killed in an accident at a crossing on the ECR's 'tramway' near Victoria Docks. The Railway was absolved of all blame since it was judged that the son had acted incautiously.

A long-running legal battle was fought over the question of the Stowmarket level-crossings – where they are still a problem to this day. The crossings were close to the station and some sidings, so road traffic was frequently held up by trains which had stopped or were shunting. Cases were brought against the GER at the County Court and twice at the Petty Sessions during the early 1870s. A hearing in November 1874 was the fourth on the subject, with a Mr Roberts being accused of 'harassing' the GER over the issue. This time the position of a goods train on the crossings whilst the engines took water set the scene for a complicated legal battle involving much quoting of clauses from the Ipswich & Bury Railway Act; this Company had built the first line through Stowmarket, which later became part of the Norwich main line. The really burning question could almost have been a riddle: when are crossing gates 'shut'? When they are across the road, or when they are across the railway? Clearly no one could decide, for the case was thrown out with each side to pay costs.

The GER was at one time famous for the rather curious branch lines which filled odd corners of East Anglia. In later years the best known of these lines was the Wisbech & Upwell Tramway, which ran alongside the roadway for much of its course.

This line was opened throughout in 1884, restricted by severe Board of Trade regulations. Maximum speed was to be 12 mph whilst locomotives were to be 'free from noise produced by blast and from the clatter of machinery, such as to constitute any reasonable ground of complaint.' None the less the tram engines seem to have scared horses regularly, beginning on the line's opening day when a horse belonging to the rival Midland Railway bolted through a hedge into a garden. According to a story in the *Railway Magazine* in 1899, two GER horses which encountered the tram on the same day were not in the least bit worried by it. The moral of the tale, apparently, was that the Midland horse shouldn't have been 'raiding' GER territory.

Sometimes the Tramway became involved in legal arguments over horses. A horse belonging to a Mr Green was frightened by a tram engine and sustained injury, so he took the GER to court in Wisbech claiming that bye-laws had been broken. The Court found that the locomotive had been guilty of 'negligent emission' of too much smoke and steam, thus breaking the Board of Trade regulations. Green was awarded £30 damages, but the GER clearly saw this as a test case and appealed. The case went through five stages, culminating in the High Court of Justice where Green was awarded damages of £40 in 1894. One wonders how many years' profits of the Tramway were swallowed up in the GER's legal fees!

Stations and Places

7.1 Melancholy Places

Two of the characteristics often assigned to stations of the GER were that the GER had many stations remote from the places they purported to serve, and that it had stations where no other Railway would have considered it worthwhile. Such problems of course were enshrined poetically:

> Melancholy places where none but Great Eastern trains deign to stop,
> And there's no one to pick up and no one to drop . . .

However the lines of the GER did become well known for elegant and handsome station buildings – the Cambridge line and the Ipswich & Bury being especially noteworthy, while the GER made its own contribution by rebuilding Norwich Thorpe in 1886 and through the dramatic extension from Bishopsgate to Liverpool Street.

Perhaps the two problems of isolation and lack of use were related, for when the various constituents of the GER were building their lines they somehow managed to avoid some of the main centres of population, perhaps appending a 'Road' to the station's name as an apology for their failure. Nowhere was this more apparent than on the original Norwich main line's Ely to Norwich section.

The first station out of Ely was originally known as 'Mildenhall Road', a spot so remote that it was ideal for the sort of illegal activities described elsewhere in this book. Located on the edge of an especially desolate stretch of fenland, the station was fully six miles from the town it claimed to serve and was, in any case, closer to Littleport! At least the next station, Laken Heath, was only about two miles from the settlement it 'served'.

In gentle terrain, Harling Road station was about two miles

from its settlement, though the 1851 ECR Guide referred to the intervening space as 'a short distance'. The author of the Guide, presumably, did not have to carry his baggage to Harling! Perhaps it was just that the railway's engineer felt Harling was not worth the effort, for the Guide described it as a 'small market

Figure 7.1   *Wenden Station, later called Audley End*
Illustrated London News, 2 August 1845

town . . . now fallen into a declining state, and there is but little traffic of any kind.'

The next station was Eccles Road, on which the Guide was able to comment that 'the village of the same name was adjacent'. 'Eccles' was close by, but it consisted of little more than a church and the Hall. 'Eccles Road' soon became bigger than Eccles! Less successful still was Spink's Lane, in the middle of nowhere between Wymondham and Hethersett; it opened on 30 July 1845 and closed in November.

Similar great achievements were accomplished between Ely and March. Black Bank station was intended to serve Downham, but fully deserved its reputation as one of the most isolated and depressing postings on the GER. Manea avoided its

Figure 7.2 *Cavendish Station, on the cross-country Cambridge to Colchester route, about 1910*
Suffolk County Council

village by only a mile and, since the villagers had no alternative route to Ely because of Vermuyden's drainage works, became a tolerably successful station. But Stonea! Fully four miles from the nearest 'village', it served a scattered handful of remote Fenland farms.

Stonea may have been fancied as the 'melancholy place' that inspired the poem, but its position must be challenged by Berney Arms which is also – quite amazingly – still open today. Halfway between Reedham and Yarmouth, Berney Arms owes its existence to an agreement of 6 June 1843 between the Yarmouth & Norwich Railway and the local landowner, Berney. He agreed to sell his land at a reasonable rate providing the Railway Company would maintain a station there in perpetuity.

Berney Arms station was duly built and opened, with a few scheduled trains, but in 1845 the Yarmouth & Norwich became part of the Norfolk Railway, which was distressed at the station's lack of traffic – hardly surprising, since there wasn't even a road to it! The only buildings nearby were windmills and a pub, and the pub existed largely for the use of the men crewing the wherries on the nearby river.

In 1850 the Norfolk Railway decided to stop its trains halting at Berney Arms on the grounds that the agreement of 1843 had specified a station but said nothing about a train. This led to a legal confrontation that lasted until 1860, ending with the NR agreeing to stop one train each way on Mondays, Wednesdays, and Saturdays, and Berney gained £200 compensation. Services, in fact, were restarted in 1855. Trains still stop there today and the service is quite luxurious compared to what it was!

7.2 Boreham and Other Private Stopping Places

The passenger trains which began running beyond Brentwood to Colchester on 29 March 1843 passed close to Boreham House, the home of Sir John Tyssen Tyrell, about three miles north-east of Chelmsford. In August Tyrell asked the ECR to allow trains to take up and set down himself and his family. This request was politely rejected, but it is clear that Tyrell began to exercise such a privilege almost immediately, for many years later (1859) he wrote to the chairman, Horatio Love:

> The putting up a flag at a moment's notice, and the time occasioned in the delay of a train never exceeded five minutes, seldom more than three, and in twenty years there has never been a train nearer than a quarter of an hour after one being stopped.

He went on to say that the privilege had been granted because he had 'saved the Eastern Counties Rail some £13,000 in hard money' – presumably by abating an initially extravagant claim for compensation.

In March 1859 the Traffic Committee discussed the practice of stopping trains at Boreham level-crossing, and recommended the construction of short platforms with signals and the appointment of an attendant, £15 of whose annual wages were to be paid by Sir John.

Clearly, for 16 years there had been no station, or formal arrangements for safety or convenience, at Boreham crossing. There followed negotiations concerning the notice Tyrell was to give (no more hailing trains like taxicabs) and the limitation of the privilege to his own lifetime. Agreement was reached but there was still no apparent hurry – in November the Committee once more resolved to construct the platforms, the signals and (perhaps as a *douceur*) 'the hut [to be] rendered suitable for habitation'.

We might begin to wonder if indeed the 'station' ever did materialise, except that in 1874 two bare platforms east of the level crossing, each about 80 feet long, with one signal post on the down side, appeared on the Ordnance Survey plan prepared in that year.

Sir John Tyrell died on 19 September 1877. No move was made against the tiny station before the funeral, but the next morning it was removed by a gang of workmen. Even its last moments are mysterious, however, for in an article in the *Essex Review*, 1925, the writer refers to 'the work of demolition' seen by a friend from a passing train, and adds that 'if my recollection

Figure 7.3 *Littleport Station*   Cambridgeshire Libraries

of the station is correct, it was a small wooden building, about the size of an . . . hen-house, and of no greater architectural merit'. Presumably this building was the hut mentioned above, but the O.S. plan does not show it, so it seems that either Captain Pilleau of the Royal Engineers missed it, or it was constructed between 1874 and 1877: the former explanation seems most likely.

Even the ghost of Boreham station lingered on, like the grin of the Cheshire cat. An article concerning Henry Ford (*Sunday Telegraph Magazine*, April 1979) described how the up boat train in which he was travelling in 1930 stopped 'at a deserted platform. It was Boreham Halt . . . ' The writer advised that the reference was the result of local investigation, and that although there may not have been a platform, it was still regarded locally as a halt because trains tended to slow or stop there. In October 1979 the ghost had, possibly, exerted this compulsion to stop so strongly upon a diesel locomotive that it had left the up line and was heeled well over, as if prepared for a long stay.

The case of Boreham was not singular. In September 1854 the ECR Officers Committee began to consider the privileges of

Figure 7.4   *The Royal Train near Harold Wood, about 1910*   Colchester Library

stopping trains claimed by Sir John Tyrell, Lord Roden, 'and others', but they did not get beyond asking the coaching superintendent to find out 'what privileges exist and upon what right they are claimed'. This was towards the close of Waddington's chairmanship, so a certain amount of doubt and confusion is not surprising.

The officers still seemed to lack a definitive list in July 1855, when they referred to the 'present practice of stopping passenger trains at Keswick Gate [Keswick is near Norwich, on the Brandon line] and other places not provided for in time-tables for the accommodation of Sir John Boileau, Mr Birkbeck and other private families – 'causing such delay'. They asked the directors to withdraw the privileges unless provided for legally.

After the GER was formed yet another case came to light. Lord William Powlett had been granted the right of stopping trains at Sexton Gate in August 1848. In 1850, the company having no record of the matter and he being unable to find the letter concerned, the privilege was withdrawn. Fourteen years later, the letter surfaced, and the Traffic Committee had little alternative than to grant him permission to stop any train except an express, on notice being given to the Superintendent. Sexton Gate has not been located, but Norfolk is indicated.

Only in the case of Boreham do we know that platforms, signals and other facilities were provided, but clearly this is an interesting by-way of railway history which awaits further investigation.

7.3   A Central Station for Cambridge?

It was not only the Mildenhalls and Harlings that suffered from stations that were out of the way, but some of the major East Anglian towns too. This was not always the fault of the Railway – Cambridge University feared the trains would infect its students with moral vices, while Saffron Walden failed to get a convenient station because of Lord Braybrooke's influence and fears for his Audley End estate. The first Colchester station was a mile north of the town due to the location of Colchester on a ridge, and later attempts by the ECR to build a new station in Crouch Street were blocked by the Tendring Hundred Railway, for example in 1862. Ely and March also had poorly-sited stations. At least Norwich had two stations, Thorpe and Victoria, though neither of them especially central. When the GER was formed Norwich Corporation feared that one would be closed and section 178 of the Amalgamation Act specified that Victoria station (sometimes known as 'the Loup' according to the *Railway Times*) had to be maintained in use. However, it suffered a reduced service, the cause of much complaint, and finally closed to passengers as a wartime economy on 22 May 1916. A third Norwich station, City, opened in 1882 by the M&GNJR, was also beyond the limits of the former city wall.

When George Hudson visited Cambridge he was not impressed by the site of its station. 'He was astonished to find the station where it was. That was not the way they did things in his part of the country.' Alderman Fawcett thought that the station was 'little better than a road-side station' and plans by the Midland & Eastern Counties Company for a new line into the 'heart of the town' were greeted enthusiastically in 1845.

A committee was formed to study the various 'Railway Mania' schemes and reported on 13 January 1846 in favour of a central station near the gaol at the edge of the town's central area. Various Companies had their own ideas, with the Cambridge & Oxford proposing two termini, though the idea for a station at Sheep's Green horrified the fellows of Peterhouse College.

A second public meeting was held on 23 January 1846, but was attended by only 60 people, probably because everyone was confused by all the rival plans being proposed. A rather curious resolution was passed, accepting that there did not 'appear to be any practicable mode of obtaining a general central station at Cambridge' but there could be 'a passenger station near the Town Gaol.'

There the matter seemed to rest until in November 1846 the ECR gave notice of plans for several lines in the area south of

Figure 7.5 *Proposed new stations in Cambridge 1846–64*

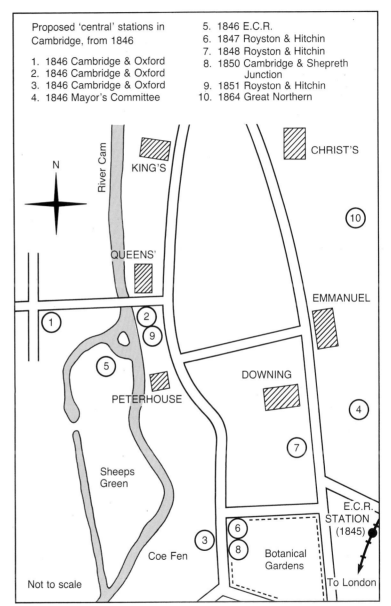

Proposed 'central' stations in Cambridge, from 1846

1. 1846 Cambridge & Oxford
2. 1846 Cambridge & Oxford
3. 1846 Cambridge & Oxford
4. 1846 Mayor's Committee
5. 1846 E.C.R.
6. 1847 Royston & Hitchin
7. 1848 Royston & Hitchin
8. 1850 Cambridge & Shepreth Junction
9. 1851 Royston & Hitchin
10. 1864 Great Northern

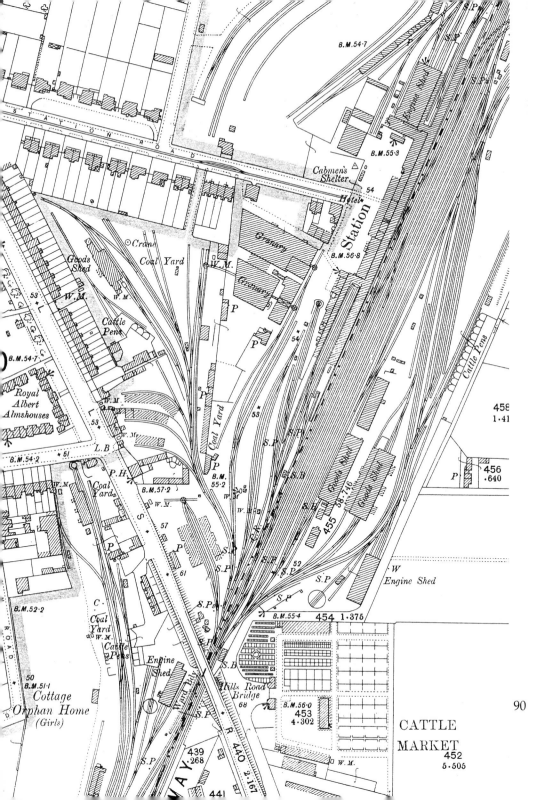

Figure 7.6 *Cambridge Station in the 1890s. Note the very long main platform (over 300 yards!), the substantial houses of Station Road, and the rail-served granary*
Ordnance Survey

Cambridge together with 'a Branch railway, to be used as a tram-road' which was to run into the town from the south across Coe Fen, and terminate at Sheep's Green. In January 1847 the Cambridge Committee reported that 'This line is intended as a town depot for goods traffic only, and is proposed to be worked by horses and not by steam power.' It would have been single track with space for a double line.

This plan provoked a furious row in Cambridge, though some joined in on minor questions such as that it would ruin a good bathing-place on the River. Councillor Balls said that

> he was not one of those disposed to annihilate the town; and if the University were disposed to act in that spirit, let them at least come forwards and compensate gentlemen for the loss of business and take their premises into their own hands. If the University were disposed to reduce the town to a collection of shopkeepers, he begged to say they were taking the right steps to carry out their views.

The University counter-attacked by painting a portrait of hundreds of barges navigating the Backs to unload at a railway wharf in front of Peterhouse. They circulated a pamphlet, arguing:

> It is earnestly hoped that all persons who feel an interest in the beauty, comfort, and property of the river Colleges will exert themselves to prevent this project from being carried into effect.

As usual, the University triumphed over the Town.

While the ECR was thus occupied, the Cambridge & Oxford was still trying for its own 'central' terminus. Several sites were proposed, including two on Sheep's Green and two near the Botanic Gardens in Trumpington Street. This threat to tranquility was solved in a different way – the line was initially authorised from Hitchin to Royston only, eventually to Shepreth. The Cambridge & Shepreth Junction scheme of 1849–50 was

90

Figure 7.7   *Cambridge Station, in Italianate style, shortly after its opening, looking*
rather unfinished   Illustrated London News, 2 August 1845

opposed by the University's MPs on the grounds that two stations would be inconvenient whilst the 1851 plan of the erstwhile Cambridge & Oxford (now Royston & Hitchin) was opposed as it would have passed 'under the windows of St Peter's College'.

In 1864 the Great Northern Railway proposed a line to terminate near Emmanuel College but this was opposed by the University and negotiations with the GER avoided the need to build a new station at all. Thus Cambridge still has an inconvenient station today, largely due to the political power of the University that could outfight a Railway Company any day!

7.4   The Three Stations of Ingatestone

Just as the population centre of a settlement can move – as it did with Eccles, under the influence of the railway – so too a station can move. Sometimes this happens quite literally, for at Chelmsford the original station was taken down in 1856 and re-erected in Broomfield Road, where it was used as railway staff accommodation until 1952. In the case of Ingatestone, it is the site of the station that has altered, and the reasons for this give us a good insight into railway history on a local scale.

In 1557 Sir William Petre, a man who had made a fortune out of the dissolution of the monasteries and spent some of it buying Ingatestone Hall, endowed a small terrace of almshouses for a priest and ten poor people. The almshouses were built in Stock Lane, to the east of the village.

In 1835–6 John Braithwaite, the ECR engineer, assisted by Charles Blacker Vignoles, was laying out the line from London to its projected terminus at Yarmouth. At Ingatestone the line chosen was to run parallel with the main road on its south side and the Parliamentary plans show that it was to enter a cutting, passing under Stock Lane between the eastern end of the almshouses and an isolated cottage occupied by one Rolf.

The construction of the ECR was protracted, reaching Brentwood in mid 1840 and then progressing very slowly towards Colchester. The then Lord Petre, who owned much land around Ingatestone and Brentwood, feared 'irreparable mischief' could be done by the navvies. In fact at Ingatestone, where 34 navvies were based in 1841, disorders were limited to minor scuffles on pay nights and the navvies ran away if the Police intervened.

Lord Petre had had a long argument with the ECR over the compensation he should get for the line crossing his lands. Though the case has been cited in the past as an example of a rapacious landowner trying to fleece a Railway, Petre maintained that his vast claim for £120,000 was an attempt to get the ECR to take a more northerly route via Writtle so that lands in which he had invested much money would be left undisturbed. This would have left Petre's home at Thorndon Hall in reasonable peace. The ECR agreed to seek Parliamentary powers for the more northerly route but failed to do so, and they then refused to pay Petre's inflated price for the original route. A legal battle ended in victory for Lord Petre.

By 1840 work was progressing at Ingatestone and Stock Lane with its almshouses could not survive in peace much longer. The almshouses, which for nearly three centuries had sheltered those on whom Fortune had failed to smile, became ECR property and Petre erected twelve new almshouses at a cost of £1,200 on the main road – paid for by the ECR, of course. The Company was struggling financially and had to make economies, one of which was to have only a level-crossing on the lane leading to Ingatestone Hall, and not a bridge; Petre agreed to this on condition that a crossing-keeper was appointed.

The extension from Brentwood to Colchester was opened for goods traffic on 7 March 1843, and for passengers on 29 March, using the five-foot gauge chosen by Braithwaite. It had to be converted to standard gauge in September and October 1844, another example of the costly yet endearing eccentricity of the ECR.

The ECR decided to have its Ingatestone station at the point where Stock Lane crossed, even though the line was in a deep cutting at this point: the site was chosen as it was nearer to the main part of the town than Hall Lane and on the only all-weather road from Stock and the hamlets situated to the east of Ingatestone. The fact that the railway was in a deep cutting at this point seems to have been a small consideration with the townsfolk, who also favoured the site. Lord Petre, however, thought the station ought to be in Hall Lane; he secured an injunction for the removal of the wooden steps down the embankment and the platform which the ECR had provided.

Although the ECR timetable for 12 July 1843 lists Ingatestone, no trains are shown as stopping there. An account written in 1925 reports the local tradition that

> At first . . . a small wooden platform, long since demolished, in the cutting half a mile or so north of the present station, served to receive passengers, while a couple of tiny brick cottages, still standing on top of the embankment, served as booking office and station.

One of the customers was the Rector of Fryerning, who

> saw the passing of the old stage coach and the coming of the railway with its first station in Stock Lane, to approach which it was necessary to descend a steep flight of steps, down which Rector Price, when old and infirm, would ride on his old grey pony.

The strangest thing about this little station must surely be that the cottages which formed its buildings at road level are now listed buildings, for three of the almshouses survived and a door was made in the end wall nearest the railway as an entrance to the ticket office.

The account of 1925 continues:

> Later, apparently, a small wooden station was erected at the site of the present station, but this must have served for a very short time only and have been removed a year or so later, when the present station was built. Unless appearances are deceptive, however, it still exists in the small building, now used as a store-shed, which stands close beside the line, at the road crossing and a few yards only south of its original site. The style of the weather-boarding of which it is constructed so closely resembles that of old Chelmsford station . . . that one cannot doubt it was built about the same time, by the same builder, to serve the same purpose.

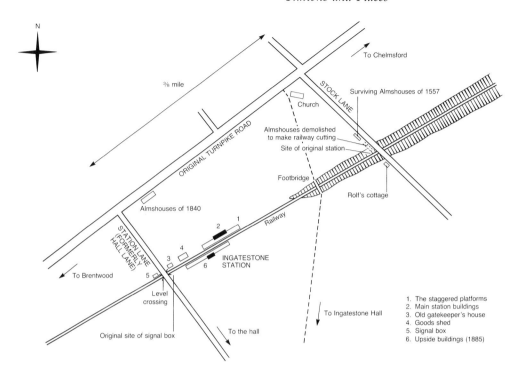

Figure 7.8 *Sketch map of Ingatestone in about 1900, showing the development of the stations*
After Ordnance Survey

This second station was replaced by a permanent red brick and stone structure in Tudor style probably chosen to please Lord Petre. An ecclesiastical effect was included by the use of pointed stone doorways, heavy doors and leaded diamond windows. The station was built in 1846 and it has been said that a red brick house to the north of the station was built at the same time for use as an hotel.

In January 1859 the ECR Traffic Committee decided that a gas supply was to be provided at the station and 'a small pipe to be laid on to the semaphore signal'; if this last refinement was carried out, Ingatestone was very sophisticated for its time, for

*Figure 7.9   When labour was cheap! Re-erecting a footbridge at Ingatestone. This is
not the bridge linking the platforms, but the one by the level crossing which was
provided between 1874 and 1876, along with a signalbox to the south-east of the
crossing. Between 1885 and 1915 the signalbox was moved to its present site to the
north-west of the crossing, and this was probably the occasion of the photograph. As
first placed, the bridge was close to the road, but the signalman needed a clear view
so it had to be moved*   R.H.G. Thomas Coll.

in 1861 at Buckhurst Hill signalman Devlin was killed climbing
the ladder of a signal-post to extinguish the lights, and even in
the 1940s Chigwell Lane station (now Debden) was known as
'Paraffin Junction' due to its array of oil lamps.

Gas or no gas, when Measom compiled his guide to the GER
in about 1864 he wrote:

> The town of Ingatestone has fallen upon evil days. The market
> place is partly enclosed; its cattle market has entirely disap-
> peared, and a once flourishing town is now a small village.

Even by 1874 the Ordnance Survey records only a small goods
yard on the down side, two sidings into the gas works on the
same side but west of Hall Lane, and a long siding behind the
up platform. No signal box is shown, no footbridge between
the platforms, and no building is shown on the up platform
though it seems there was a small shelter.

By 1886 the stationmaster was Absalom Evans and he still
reigned in 1894, so he probably saw the introduction of slip
coaches, for from July 1890 Ingatestone was one of five stations
on the Colchester line being so served. The idea was not new,
for in September 1857 Mr Russell Ellice had asked for a carriage
to be 'detached at speed' at Broxbourne and forwarded to Hertford. The ECR rejected the idea on grounds of public safety,
but slip coaches were tried out on the Brighton line early in
1858.

Ingatestone's third station is the one we see today. It originally had staggered platforms, but these have been largely
eliminated by extensions. The old wooden station has long since
gone but a brick goods shed was built later. There is also a
Tudor-style house near the crossing, where the wooden gates
were replaced by barriers in January 1972. The ECR relied a lot
on timber and at Ingatestone even the goods crane, rated at 1½
tons, had a wooden jib.

Another unusual feature of the station, especially such a
minor one, was that it had a booking office on each platform.
The up side office was provided, it has been said, for the convenience of the Petre family when going to London; these up
offices were built between 1873 and 1895, during the same
period in which a footbridge also was constructed and
additional sidings.

Between the present station and the original site a brick footbridge crosses the line, carrying a footpath towards the Hall.
At about 16 feet wide it is much grander than a pedestrian
would require, and was perhaps intended to take coaches to
the Hall.

The three surviving alms cottages have been turned into two
and close to them the GER added some cottages for its workers

in 1902. Thus it can be seen that the railway history of what appears at first sight to be little more than a wayside station involves a lot of development and change.

As a footnote to the story of Ingatestone station, it is interesting that Henry Labouchere inherited the nearby Hylands estate from his father and sold it, but found that, whereas £35,000 had been insisted on previously for land and compensation assessed at £4,000 by local valuers empanelled by the company, the devaluation of the land had been much less than expected. He contacted the ECR by a letter of 3 December 1839 to its Chairman, Henry Bosanquet, and voluntarily relinquished £15,000 of the amount due from the ECR; the ECR directors praised Labouchere's action as 'noble' and 'honourable'. Labouchere had much contact with railways since he was Vice-President of the Board of Trade from 1835 to 1839, and then became its President until 1841.

7.5 Hatfield Peverel: 'The Railway Passes Through'

Hatfield Peverel is a modest village, formerly on the main road to Harwich and a stopping point for coaches. The station, too, is modest enough; a small range of antiquated offices on the up platform – an observer might think they had been there since the opening day, but he would be wrong!

The extension to Colchester opened in 1843 but that July's timetable shows no station at Hatfield Peverel. It has been stated that the station opened in 1844 and it is listed in *Bradshaw* for January 1845; it was certainly operating by 1845 for the ECR Traffic Committee inspected it and resolved

> There being no accommodation whatever for passenger traffic at this station, that the plan proposed by Mr Wood for this station be adopted and an estimate be submitted. That the road to the station be ballasted.

When the Committee reached Marks Tey they found the same state of affairs and resolved 'that a similar station be erected here to that proposed at Hatfield.' It was not unusual for a

station to be opened without proper buildings; often a nearby house became a booking office, or a small wooden hut was provided.

By 1848 the village definitely had a station, known simply as 'Hatfield', and with a stationmaster called Isaac Flory. His work cannot have been great as the train service seems to have been twice a day in each direction. Hopes for the growth of traffic, however, quite literally, 'went up in smoke'.

Fire destroyed the station in February 1849, probably very quickly as it was likely to have been of wood. The ECR seem to have felt that the village did not deserve another station, for on 23 February the *Essex Standard* noted: 'The ECR have intimated their intention to discontinue Hatfield station on and after 1 March.' So it was not rebuilt, and in December 1858 the

Figure 7.10   Hatfield Peverel Station around 1900. The signalbox is on the up side with the 'principal buildings'. There is no canopy on that side but there were small waiting rooms and an open-fronted covered area. The station was opened in 1878
Fred Spalding; D. Thompson Coll.

ECR refused even to open a 'flag station' at the village. County directories for 1851, 1855, and 1859 comment sourly of Hatfield Peverel: 'The Eastern Counties Railway passes through.' White's Directory of 1862, published in Sheffield, referred to a station in the village, so perhaps the sad news travelled only slowly, or Hatfield Peverel kept its shame as quiet as possible, for in 1862 a place without a station was a poor place indeed . . . and to be on a line that 'passed through' only was highly humiliating!

The only person in the district who did not suffer inconvenience was Sir John Tyrell who lived at Boreham House, between Hatfield and Chelmsford. As we have seen, until his death in 1877 he had the right to flag down any train he wished to travel on at his own private Boreham station.

It seems likely that the removal of the private platform at Boreham in 1877 and the opening of a new Hatfield Peverel station on 1 March 1878 were connected. Perhaps the Tyrell family had more influence over the GER than the denizens of benighted Hatfield, and with the end of their 'droit de seigneur' the GER were able to secure a new station elsewhere. But Hatfield Peverel never became a very grand station and it is still little more than a wayside halt.

7.6 Braintree: How the Railway Changed a Town

Although a visionary scheme of 1825 had proposed a railway from Braintree to Colchester, the small Essex 'twin towns' of Braintree and Bocking were missed by the ECR when it opened in 1843. A substantial interest in a branch line to fill the needs of the district being aroused, a meeting was held at Witham in March 1845 and the Maldon, Witham & Braintree Railway was launched. This railway had a great impact on Braintree, causing its triumph over the long-time rival of Bocking, and rescuing it from economic gloom.

The region was in a miserable economic state after its principal trade, woollen cloth, had been devastated by the Napoleonic Wars and by Yorkshire competition. Much of the capital for the

MW&B was subscribed from outside the area, but whereas 28 Maldon people promised to subscribe an average of £406 each, four Bocking people £1,575 each and 19 at Witham £1,307 each, nobody from Braintree subscribed anything! Notable subscribers included Samuel Courtauld, the Bocking silk manufacturer, and a number of landowners. Also significant were Maldon merchants, concerned to revive the trade of their port.

Farmers in the district saw that a railway would benefit them. The prospectus claimed that 'the district to be served by the railway is one of the most important both for corn and cattle in the kingdom.' It would help to develop Maldon as a port to handle 'the supply of coal, timber, and slate, and . . . salt, lime, chalk and oil cake.' The cost of all these articles would be reduced considerably, stimulating local industry and agriculture; lime, of course, was used for fertiliser, but so also would be the horse manure that the railways carried out into the country from the streets of London.

Goods trains started running on the line in September 1848, with 300 tons of coal and 350 tons of other freight carried that month. The first passenger train ran on 2 October 1848, with a special excursion being put on within a few days for the Braintree Fair.

By 1851 the ECR Guide was able to speak of Braintree as 'an improving market town', also that 'it has been considerably improved on its south eastern side, since the railway has been brought into it, by the erection of a very handsome station, for which a new road has been formed.' The road was created by extending the former 'Dead Lane' and calling it 'Railway Street'.

The effect of the railway on the town was considerable. Having experienced a stagnant population since 1801, it rose from 3,670 in 1841 to 6,168 by 1911, yet neighbouring Bocking – with no railway station of its own – rose only from 3,437 to 3,448. How did the railway cause such a reversal in the town's downward fortunes?

Firstly, the effects of the railway were not always beneficial. The town's cattle trade was boosted by the improved transport with weekly sales, but the October Fair – to which as many as

Figure 7.11   *Braintree's Railway Street area in about 1910, showing the effects of 50 years of railway-influenced development. In the south-west corner can be seen the second station of 1869 on the Dunmow extension, with north of that the sidings for the brick and tile works. The first station was close to the Goods Shed, just to the east of Railway Street. Along this street can be seen Young's brewery, the Sun inn used by the carriers, and to its west the streets of terraced houses built after the arrival of the railway using slate brought in by train. 'Manor Works' was the home of Crittall's, who also had a factory beside the line in Witham. On the south side of Manor Street can be seen the malthouse of Ridley & Co, the town's Gas Works, and the foundry of Messrs Lake & Elliott. Thus the arrival of the railway had the effect of creating a quite distinct industrial quarter in Braintree*   Ordnance Survey

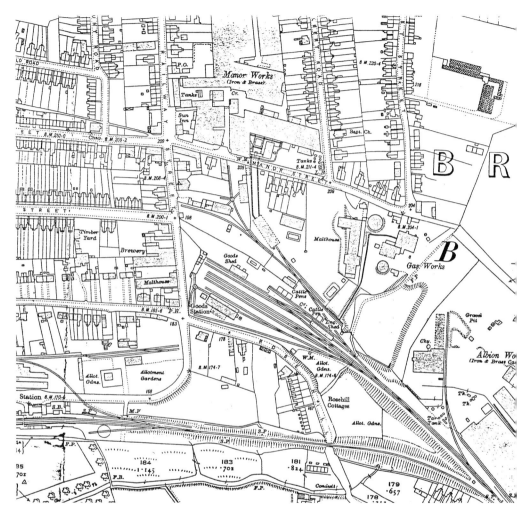

20,000 sheep had once been brought by drovers – was finished; it became an event merely for the sale of cattle and hops. The May Fair declined too, by 1870 being described as 'little more than a toy fair'.

Other people who suffered included the coach proprietors, though at first they adapted themselves to the railways. In 1830 Braintree was on the through route from London to Bury and some coaches ran as far as Norwich. By 1845 Norwich to London coaches were few, and most coaches ran only to the railway in Chelmsford. 'The Wonder' ran from Chelmsford to Bury, though 'The Phenomena' still ran to Norwich and a Mr Hayward put on a service from Chelmsford to Clare via Braintree.

The carriers of goods were more resilient to the railways in 1845. Ephraim Salter ran from the Woolpack in Bocking and forwarded his goods to London by rail from Chelmsford; several other carriers still ran to Aldgate and Lime Street in the City. There was still a carrier to Norwich every day.

But by 1870 the coach proprietors were finished, the only survivor being the White Hart coach from Bocking to Braintree's Horn Inn to connect with the trains. The carriers had adapted though, most of them making inns near the station their base – the Railway Tavern and the Sun being their favourites. Carriers ran to Stebbing, Saffron Walden, Halstead, Felsted, Dunmow, Cavendish, Sudbury, Toppesfield, and Chelmsford, indicating Braintree's importance as a 'railhead'.

The arrival of the railway caused a proliferation of coal mer-chants since the reduced prices made coal much more in demand. Before 1848 the town only had one coal merchant, by 1870 it had at least four, and in 1900 there were eight in Railway Street alone. In 1851 a mutual coal club was formed and bought Durham coal at 18s a ton. To help in the supply of coal, the

Figure 7.12 *The Braintree line in April 1910. Y65 Class No. 1304 heads the 3.37 pm to Braintree away from Witham*   Essex Libraries

Gas Works was moved nearer to the railway yard in Manor Street.

Also boosted was the corn trade, helped by the inward supply of fertiliser and the ease of outward movement. The one corn dealer and three maltsters of 1845 rose within ten years to four corn factors, six corn millers and a large number of bakers and flour dealers. Young's opened a brewery opposite the goods yard and Ridley's built maltings alongside it in about 1854.

Heavier industry also became possible. The window manufacturer, Francis Crittall, relocated to Manor Street, beside the railway, in 1893 whilst Lake & Elliott opened their works in 1906; this had its own sidings. There was also a brick and tile works beside Braintree's second station, opened when the line was extended to Great Dunmow and Bishop's Stortford in 1869.

During the Victorian period Braintree grew very rapidly on its south-eastern side with several new streets being built to fill the space between the town centre and the railway. Many of the new houses in Manor Street and Victoria Street were roofed with slate, brought in for the first time by rail.

The railway was also a direct boost to employment. By 1851 eight railway workers lived in Mill Lane, including a stoker, a fitter, a driver, an engine cleaner, a labourer, and three porters. A guard lived in Railway Street and another in Manor Street, where also an agent and a clerk could be found.

So the effect of the railway on a small East Anglian town was quite considerable, even before it came within the field of commuters. The same effects could be found in most of the market towns on the Great Eastern system, which was why towns that did not have a railway were so desperate to gain one.

8

Great Eastern Horse Power

The first recorded railway in England is dated to *c.*1603–4, near Nottingham. The first steam locomotive to be put on a railway did not turn its wheels until 1804. During the intervening two centuries railways relied almost entirely upon the horse; even after the advent of the steam locomotive, horses continued to be used for many tasks including shunting and, of course, deliveries by road.

On several occasions short branch lines with meagre traffic were worked almost entirely by horse; this was especially the case if there was no passenger service. It was quite unusual, however, for a passenger service once worked by steam engines to be taken over by horses. This rather embarrassing fate befell the St Ives and Huntingdon line of the East Anglian Railways in 1849; traffic was so sparse that the Eastern Counties was no longer prepared to operate a steam service.

Faced with the prospect of an expensively-built line going out of use, the EAR chose an unusual remedy. The carriage foreman at the Company's Lynn base, Mr Little, was instructed to design a vehicle to be pulled by a horse. This was then built, with a capacity of 60 passengers of all three classes, though some of the passengers and the guard were accommodated on the roof. The guard also had a powerful handbrake.

The driver of this strange 'train' had a special appliance to allow him to uncouple the horse in an 'emergency'. It was intended that this contraption should travel at up to 15 mph, but it was clearly too slow since the Railway Commissioners objected that the legal requirement of an average 12 mph for Parliamentary trains was not being kept.

The small Essex market town of Coggeshall nearly became another place to be served by horse-power. Its populace was rather disgruntled at being off the ECR main line, which passed through Kelvedon three miles away. Several schemes were put

forward for a Coggeshall branch, but at least one of these was killed off by the ECR's insistence that a Coggeshall branch would only provide enough traffic to occupy a horse. Insulted by this, the Coggeshall people withdrew their scheme.

Shunting was probably the most dangerous occupation for railway horses, thus in December 1854 horse number 409 was reported as killed on the line at Chelmsford. On 22 May 1858 horseman Sparrow and his horse were killed at Stowmarket under the wheels of a special coal train. Only after the latter incident was it decided to issue a circular to all ECR station-masters desiring them to cease shunting when a special train was due.

The large horse population of a railway like the ECR required housing and feeding, both at considerable expense. However,

Figure 8.1   *Shunting by horse at March Station in about 1905. Trains for Peterborough, Doncaster, London, Cambridge (via Chatteris), and Hunstanton are indicated*   Cambridgeshire Libraries

Figure 8.2   *Trowse Station. The small wooden goods shed is of interest and the tall, lower quadrant signals*   Norfolk Libraries

such was the nature of ECR territory that large stocks of horses were only needed in London and Norwich; most stations had just one or two. In August 1855 it was reported that the two horses at Fakenham and the one at Shelford were being put up at public houses, and so proper railway stables were needed; the stables at Trowse needed extending in order to accommodate two horses!

In December 1854 it was reported that four horses had been bought from Lucas Brothers of Lowestoft, where they had been building coke ovens for the ECR. The horses cost £41 and £36, two going at each price. At the same time four horses were reported as sold at £18 9s, being 'worn out and quite useless to the company.' The Cab Superintendent reported that he had

sold three horses for £18 10s; they had been bought for £76 4s only a year earlier, a rate of depreciation extraordinary even for the ECR, so it was ruled that horse sales were only to be made by the Company Storekeeper in future. It would seem that a lucrative little racket had been nipped in the bud.

The ECR had a strong interest in horses of another kind since it served Newmarket, where seasonal race traffic could be highly profitable. Horse-racing seems to have been one of the first sports to be commercially sponsored, and in 1854 the ECR was persuaded to give £100 to promote a new race at Newmarket. This was quite a considerable sum, and the ECR was pressurised into providing the same money the next year!

Sinclair, the locomotive engineer of the ECR in 1859, clearly felt that horses were less than ideal for shunting; in November of that year he recommended the construction of 'small and inexpensive but powerful engines . . . for shunting purposes for the use of stations.' He believed these would cost only a third of the price of the engines in use, and would also replace the horses. However, horses were much more economic for shunting at wayside stations, and tramped the goods sidings of East Anglia for many years after the demise of Sinclair.

In November 1864 the GER Stores Committee referred to the Brick Lane stables and hospital for sick horses. It was noted that the horses worked for 15 to 16 hours a day and 'no more could be got out of them' (note the unusually compassionate tone). If such hours seem cruelly long, it should be noted that two years before, after a driver had been sacked for causing a slight accident at Fenchurch Street, it was resolved that no driver should work more than 16 hours 'except in emergency'.

The GER Traffic Committee noted in its Minutes a wide variety of equine statistics. In the six months ending 31 December 1866 the 'stock on hand' was 525 horses; 89 had been purchased during the year at an average price of £37 4s but four had been killed in accidents, 28 had become 'worn out', and 14 had died or been put down due to disease.

Figure 8.3   (*On facing page*) *The enormous Stratford Works of the GER about 1900. Waddington Street commemorates the former ECR Chairman*   Ordnance Survey

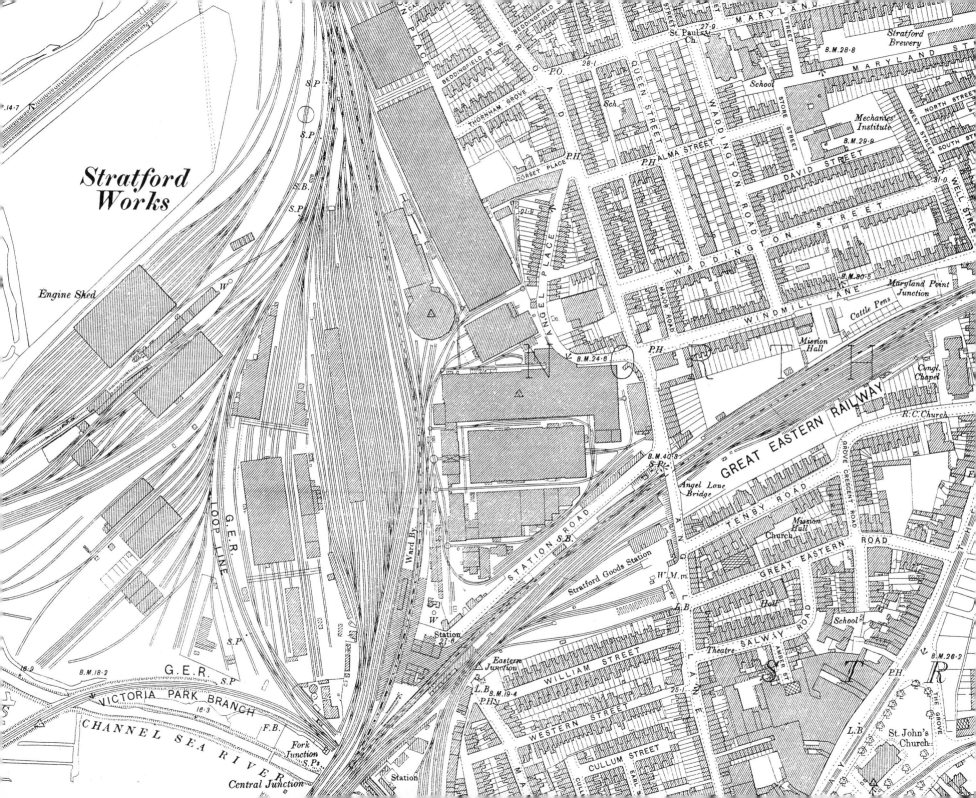

Stratford
Works

Engine Shed

S.P.

S.P.

S.B.

S.P.

W

S.P.

G.E.R. LOOP LINE

S.P.

G.E.R.

B.M.18·2   S.P.

16·9

VICTORIA PARK BRANCH   16·3

CHANNEL SEA RIVER   F.B.

Fork
Junction
S.Ps.

Central Junction

Station

Ward By.

Station
27·6

W

W

Station S.B.

STATION ROAD

BEDDINGFIELD ST.

THORNHAM GROVE

Sch.

PH.

DORSET PLACE

91·9

ANGEL PLACE

N

B.M.24·6

PH.

ROAD

St. Paul's St
Ch.

27·9

28·1

P.O.

Sch.

P.H.

QUEEN STREET

ALMA STREET

MAJOR ROAD

MARYLAND

STREET

Stratford
Brewery

B.M.28·8

MARYLAND ST.

School

WADDINGTON ROAD

STORE STREET

WEST STREET

NORTH STREET

SOUTH ST.

Mechanics
Institute

B.M.29·9

DAVID STREET

31·0

WELL STREET

B.M.30·5

WINDMILL LANE

Maryland Point
Junction

Cattle Pens

Mission Hall

PH.

N

B.M.40·3
S.P.

Angel Lane
Bridge

Cong.l
Chapel

R.C.Church

GREAT EASTERN RAILWAY

TENBY ROAD

Mission
Hall

GROVE CRESCENT ROAD

Church

GREAT EASTERN

ROAD

SALWAY ROAD

AMBER ST

School

GROVE

B.M.26·2

Stratford Goods Station

W.m

Eastern
Junction

L.B.

L.B. B.M.19·4
P.H.

WILLIAM STREET

WESTERN STREET

CULLUM STREET

EARL ST

Hall

Theatre

S

ANGEL LANE

25·1

T

PH.

R

THE

L.B.

St. John's
Church

Like its locomotives, the GER horses were identified officially by numbers; thus in 1865 it was recorded that 'Roan mare no. 1161 having diseased lungs was sold to the knackers.' No. 903 died at Cambridge and 'Gray horse no. 1148, whilst shunting trucks at Witham, fell into the engine pit, breaking its hind leg in two places, and had to be killed.' No doubt the horses acquired their own unofficial names as well; many of the railway men would have come from country districts and it is hard to imagine them calling out, 'Whoa there, number 1254!'

The men who worked with the horses were a fairly colourful lot. The GER staff records for 1892–3 contain a number of references to 'Carmen' being punished for various misdemeanours. Carman Hall was driving through Hackney Road when he saw a policeman take a drunk into custody; Hall made an attempt to rescue the drunk, but was himself arrested and locked up overnight. The Magistrates were not amused and fined him 20s; the GER suspended him for four days. Carman Lomas suffered the ultimate punishment of being 'discharged'; his offence was

to make a fraudulent claim on the GER accident fund when his real problem was that he was 'suffering from the results of venereal disease.'

Carman Booker allowed a horse belonging to the Great Western Railway to nibble some oysters that were part of his own load; he was fined half a day's pay. Mounted Messenger Sparks was even more careless – he allowed his pony to fall through an open cellar flap, costing him a whole day's pay.

The peak of GER horse-power came in the years before World War I. In 1911 the GER had five major stables in the London area alone. Biggest of these was at Hare Street, Bethnal Green, with 436 horses. The others included Quaker Street with 108, Spitalfields and Devonshire Street with 104 each, and Cambridge Heath with 96. The horse 'Infirmary' was still in operation, with 123 places. Altogether the GER had 1,750 horses in this period, of which the heaviest was the Bishop's Stortford 'shunter', weighing 1 ton ¾ cwt.

With the increased use of motor delivery lorries in the towns and the declining use of country sidings, the railway horse came to the end of its career. In 1922 the GER had 282 shunting

Figure 8.4 *Chelmsford Viaduct in September 1911, with S46 Class 4–4–0 hauling the 1.50 pm Lowestoft to Liverpool Street*   LCGB K. Nunn Coll.

horses alone, but by 1967 there was only one left in the entire country. This was 'Charlie' who, appropriately, worked at Newmarket. An era came to an end when he retired on 21 February 1967, spending the rest of his days in Somerset.

8.1 Dangerous Tramway: Wells-next-the-Sea

The coming of the railway to East Anglia, with its long coastline and inland ports, brought a requirement to link the new transport with the old, in the form of short branches from the main lines to the places where the small sailing vessels called. Wells is a small town with a long history and many interesting features, one of which is its peculiar relationship with the sea. The town is situated at the navigable head of a lengthy creek, and has a stone-built quay which is the principal feature of its harbour. Having reached the coast proper, there is another long channel through beaches of sand before vessels gain the open sea.

When the Wells & Fakenham Railway was opened in December 1857 the station was placed on the southern outskirts of the town, a quarter of a mile short of the harbour, well above it, and with the town in between. If the railway was to make much sense it was clearly necessary to bridge the gap between the station and the harbour, and within a few years a circuitous branch was constructed in a loop round the eastern side of the town. This line was generally termed the Wells Tramway, although the first half was an ordinary railway; it was the northern section, along the harbour, which was the tramway, and the whole line was just under a mile long.

The line was apparently completed and put into use late in 1860, for when the ECR Traffic Committee met on 2 January 1861 they discussed arrangements made with a Mr Spicer of Wells to work 'the tramway there' pro tem. Spicer was supplying two horses, one man, and a boy for 50s per week and this was approved. In spite of the equestrian pace the line had already claimed a victim, the death of farmer S. Cable being reported at the same meeting. Cable had visited the station to

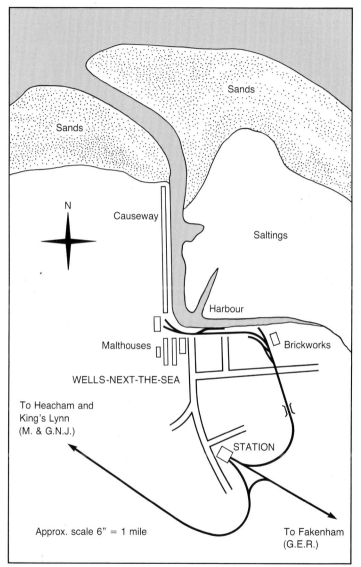

Figure 8.5 *Sketch map of Wells, showing station and tramway*
After Ordnance Survey

see two horses which Spicer had hired from him to do the work, and whilst uncoupling one of the wagons which his animals were moving, he was caught between the buffers – a cruel fate for one who, it seems, was only trying to be helpful.

The earnings of the tramway from 20 December 1860 (probably when it was brought into use – 'opened' would seem to be too grand a word in the circumstances) to 5 January were £4 14s, but by mid February Spicer found that the expenses of the work exceeded his allowance, and he asked for it to be increased to £3 weekly. The Traffic Committee did not welcome this request with open arms; perhaps they saw the thin end of a wedge, although it is difficult to imagine that Spicer was profiteering, bearing in mind that he had to hire and (probably) feed and house the horses and pay his labour. Nevertheless, the Committee asked Sinclair, the ECR engineer, what the cost of locomotive working would be and on 27 February he reported that the line was not suitable for locomotives.

In March 1861 the tramway claimed another victim, a boy named Bunting being killed when, trying to get onto one of the buffers of a wagon, he fell beneath a wheel. We do not know if he was the boy employed by Spicer, or a chance joy-rider, but the former seems likely, as the line followed a fairly remote course except along the quays which, we may assume, was a magnet for the boys of the town – and not so much for play as for work.

The receipts from the tramway for the seven weeks ending 31 March 1861 were £34 2s 9d and the expenses were £21; clearly Spicer had been given his increase, but in July it was decided to reduce his payment from £3 to £2 per week in the summer months (less coastal coal traffic to haul?) and in October 1862 the Committee increased it to £3 per week during the winter months. The concept of 'cash flow' was well in the future, but no doubt Spicer had a word – perhaps several words – for it.

The traffic at this time was mainly incoming coal and exported malt. In August 1862 the GER agreed to carry a lifeboat free to Wells for the National Lifeboat Institution, and being rail-borne thus far, it was probably taken down the tramway to reach the water. Two years previously the ECR had agreed with the NLI for the transport of a lifeboat and its carriage from London to Leiston (then the terminus of the Aldeburgh branch) at half rate.

It appears that lifeboats got a somewhat better deal than shipwrecked mariners, for in March 1858 the Traffic Committee noted that hitherto these unfortunates had been allowed to travel home free, but as the LSWR, the LNWR, and the GNR charged a halfpenny per mile, it was decided to advise the Shipwrecked Mariners Society that in future a charge of ½d per mile in third-class carriages would be made.

We leave the Wells Tramway with 90 years more to run: it was closed in 1952.

9

World War I

The first few weeks of the Great War brought unprecedented traffic to the GER. Between 5 August and 14 September 1914, 870 military trains were run – mostly to Colchester. The old station at Newmarket was converted into a bathing place for soldiers on the move by securing sheets between iron posts. Tea was provided for soldiers at Liverpool Street, price 1d a cup.

The GER formed its own ambulance train which began running between Southampton and Cambridge in September 1914. It was under the command of Lt-Surgeon Redpath and was made up of five brake third carriages, two main-line composites, one brake third and luggage van, and a first-class dining car. The brake thirds became wards with twenty beds each, the luggage van was converted into a pharmacy and operating room, and the composites provided accommodation for staff and stores. In 1915 a new ambulance train was ready, consisting of 16 carriages, weighing 440 tons. Before going into service it toured the region, being visited by 52,000 people at various centres.

Christmas 1914 brought some military traffic of an unusual nature. A Norwich express made a special stop at Forest Gate to pick up a 400 lb. Christmas cake for delivery (via Colchester) to the East Anglian Brigade, which was stationed at Lexden. The cake was cut up with a sword.

By 1915 the press was starting to experience wartime censorship and even the inoffensive *GERM* began to suffer blank pages carrying only the words 'excision by censor'. The magazine carried many reports on what had happened to Great Eastern men who had joined the forces; one had become an army major in charge of stores and transport, whilst a clerk from King's Lynn named Mendham had got no further than a camp in the asylum grounds at Colchester, from where he was

able to watch operations at the nearby station. No doubt it was a lot safer there than in Flanders!

Much excitement was caused by the setting up of a POW camp for German prisoners beside the line at Stratford.

By 1916 the system was being run with military needs given first priority all the time. Certain key structures on the GER were protected by military staff, so the GER employees in the area needed identity cards. These structures included Flordon viaduct, Lakenham viaduct, and the Wensum swing-bridge on

Figure 9.1 *A Great War cartoon from* Punch. *The billboards suggest a GER setting*

"WAR'S ALARMS"

Timorous Old Lady (in a twitter). " Are those cannon balls, station-master ? "
Station-Master (compassionately). " Oh no, mu'm, they're only Dutch cheeses, 'm', come by the Rotterdam boat last night—that's all, mu'm ! "

Figure 9.2 *Wartime traffic. A troop special from St Botolph's to Plymouth passes Thoby signalbox north of Shenfield Junction on 16 August 1914, behind T26 No. 1253*   LCGB K. Nunn Coll.

Newmarket Line

i   Fulbourne and Six Mile Bottom
ii   Six Mile Bottom and Dullingham
iii   Saxham and Bury St Edmunds

Norwich Line

i   Chesterton Junction and Waterbeach
ii   Padnal Signalbox and Shippea Hill
iii   Shippea Hill and Lakenheath
iv   Thetford West Junction and Roudham Junction
v   Roudham Junction and Harling Road
vi   Harling Road and Eccles Road
vii   Eccles Road and Attleborough
viii   Attleborough and Spooner Row
ix   Spooner Row and Wymondham

One other key change at the time was that signalboxes ceased to be a male preserve. By 1918 the GER had its first 'signalwoman' at Burnham Market.

Special Post Office telephone circuits were also set up to link key points on the GER, as shown in Figure 9.3. Many other places were on 'box to box' circuits which could cause complications: Hopton signalbox could only communicate with Lowestoft via Coke Ovens Junction box. Most of the telephones were placed in the stationmasters' offices, although a few went to the booking office, as at Thetford. South Tottenham, though, had its telephone in the 'down side waiting room'; this must have been useful for anyone who's train was late and wanted their dinner kept in the oven!

The outbreak of war coincided with an improvement in GER timetables which had been planned for some time. The October 1914 timetable included many extra 'semi-fast' services. Most of these new trains were cut out in the timetable introduced on 15 January 1917, which placed the GER in line with wartime economies. The famous 'honeymoon train', the 2.24 pm from Yarmouth to London, ceased, as did the 8.10 am from Clacton and the 8.54 am from Harwich. Two of the surviving Norwich

the Norwich main line, plus Forncett viaduct on the Forncett to Wymondham loop.

To accommodate dramatic increases of traffic along some routes, temporary 'block' signalboxes were installed on parts of the Newmarket line and the Ely to Norwich line. Permanent signals were not erected, but each box had two men with hand signals and detonators. After each train had passed they had to put down detonators and show red flags until the signalman at the 'command' box gave the 'all clear'. These temporary boxes were between the following points:

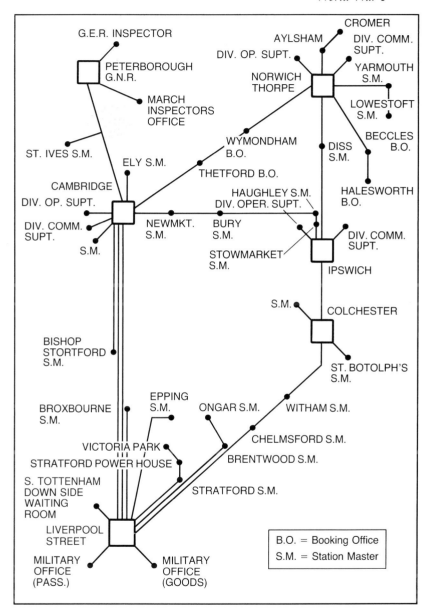

Figure 9.3 *GER Emergency Telephone Circuits, 1917. The omission of Harwich is rather surprising*

to St Pancras trains were also withdrawn. There were further major changes from 1 May 1918, notably on the Cambridge line where the slow trains were cut out and the expresses had to call at all stations north of Bishop's Stortford. Many mid-day services on the suburban lines were cut out.

More than any other railway company in World War I, the GER was involved in the struggle against Zeppelins and bomber planes. Throughout the war, GER staff monitored the passage of airships and aircraft; the results were recorded on large charts, preserved at the Public Record Office in Kew.

On the evening of 19 January 1915, stationmaster Weston at Yarmouth Vauxhall was alerted by the sound of engines. He heard bombs fall and rushed to the South station to find that several people had been killed but the GER had suffered no damage.

This marked the start of the Zeppelin campaign, with the German navigators frequently using the railway lines to guide them to their targets. The rails glimmered in the moonlight, providing help that no 'black-out' could prevent. The stationmaster at Snettisham saw an airship following the line from Heacham to Dersingham, then saw six flashes over King's Lynn. Two of these were bombs that fell at King's Lynn Junction, throwing earth over the line and slightly damaging a signal post. The stationmaster's house lost a few windows and the Royal Train shed was damaged. The crew of a shunting engine sheltered in a pit beneath their engine!

Those who suffered most on this occasion included GER staff who were at home in the town – goods clerk G. Henson lost the back of a hand and parcels clerk H. Lewis was blown out of bed. Two lines in the docks were blocked by debris. There were jokes about renaming the town 'Zeppe Lynn'.

On 16 April 1915 Zeppelins were seen all over the region from Lowestoft to Southend. Bombs were dropped at Colchester, Maldon, Braintree, Oulton Broad, Ipswich, and Bury. A GER

Figure 9.4   *0–6–2T No. 1000 prepares to leave Liverpool Street for Chingford on 20 March 1915*
                                                                LCGB K. Nunn Coll.

train near Bury was chased by a Zeppelin which dropped five bombs, but all missed. A carriage was destroyed at Lowestoft, but otherwise the GER suffered little. Driver James Goodall of Braintree picked up an incendiary bomb and immersed it in water, earning a gold watch from the local Council.

From April 1916 all sightings were recorded by the GER, with notes on bombs dropped and any Zeppelins destroyed. The resulting maps show that the Zeppelins were very inconsistent in where they chose to bomb. On 1 August 1916 they bombed Yarmouth, Norwich, and Haverhill, but other places bombed that month included Postland (deep in the Fens) and little Forncett; the railway was the only thing of military significance at both these places.

After a Zeppelin was destroyed at Lowestoft at 6.40 am on 28 November 1916, things quietened down for a while. September 1917 saw a renewed effort, but generally the Zeppelins ignored East Anglia and concentrated their attentions on London. The coast was used as a navigational aid, so that on 28 August 1917 returning Zeppelins were seen by GER staff at Billericay, Wickford, Woodbridge, and Trimley. Later in the war the Zeppelins simply followed the Thames and GER stationmasters no longer had this unusual traffic to record.

The war had a great impact on the GER services across the North Sea (which had lost its earlier title of the 'German Ocean') from Tilbury and Harwich. Harwich itself became a military base and the last passenger ferry for civilian use left it on 6 August 1914. Amongst the passengers on board the SS *St Petersburg* was Count von Bülow, the German ambassador, returning home.

The GER Hotel at Harwich became a hospital and the voices of cheerful holidaymakers became a thing of the past. All civilian services were transferred to Tilbury, which also received the first influx of Belgian refugees in September 1914. During October some more arrived at Parkeston Quay, and it was said that many of them knelt on the quayside to give thanks for their safe delivery.

Some of the GER's ships were taken over for military and naval use, but others were retained to operate a basic service to the Netherlands.

The Great War marked the introduction of submarines on a large scale, and the GER's ships were soon involved in scuffles with U-boats. On 11 December 1914 the *Colchester* was chased by a U-boat for 20 minutes before outpacing it. On 28 March 1915 the *Brussels* was attacked whilst carrying recruits from the GER, but again the U-boat failed to draw blood. That May the *Colchester* was again chased, this time when only two miles from Harwich. On 17 August a torpedo passed right underneath the *Cromer*; the U-boat then chased the ship for 20 miles before the superior speed of the *Cromer* rescued it from further danger.

This contest between the GER steamers and the U-boats gave

rise to an incident involving a GER captain that became a subject of international debate over the treatment of prisoners.

9.1 The *Brussels* Affair

Charles Fryatt was born in Southampton in 1872 but moved to Harwich whilst still a child and was educated at the Corporation School there. He naturally turned to the sea for a career since his father had been first officer on the GER's *Cambridge*. In 1892 Fryatt signed up as a seaman on the *Ipswich*, another GER vessel.

He rose to become Master of the *Colchester* and then in 1913 was placed in charge of the *Newmarket* on the Harwich to Rotterdam cargo run.

After the start of the War, Captain Fryatt was in charge of a succession of ships operating from Harwich or Tilbury to Rotterdam. In March 1915 he was commanding the *Wrexham* (on loan from the Great Central Railway) when signalled to stop by a U-boat. He ignored the signal, and steamed at 16 knots through shoals and mines in order to escape. Fryatt was rewarded with an inscribed watch for this exploit.

Barely three weeks later he was commanding the *Brussels* when another U-boat was sighted near the Maas Light Vessel. This time he could not outpace the submarine, and seemed to be in danger of being torpedoed as the U-boat submerged. Instead, Fryatt turned the *Brussels* towards the last position in which the U-boat had been sighted, hoping to ram it as it slipped beneath the waves.

There was much debate as to whether or not Fryatt succeeded in sinking the U33. There were no marks on the hull of his ship, but the Germans were evasive about what had happened to the U-boat's captain. Fryatt was rewarded with another watch and his heroism was well covered in the press. As a non-combatant, Fryatt had, however, acted unusually in trying to ram the submarine.

In June 1916 the *Brussels* left Hook of Holland with refugees on board, again under Fryatt's command. He never reached

Essex, but was reported two days later as having been captured and taken with his ship to Zeebrugge. Though subsequent events caused a sensation in Britain, the full story took several years to emerge.

It seems likely that the Germans made a deliberate attempt to capture the *Brussels* by tracking it as it left Hook. Fryatt and his ship were intercepted by five destroyers and torpedo boats at 1.30 am on 3 June 1916. Armed German seamen clambered aboard and smashed the ship's radio. Most of the English crew were taken off and the Germans installed their own commander. When they rang down to the engine-room for the *Brussels* to start, there was no response – they had forgotten that the engine-room crew had been taken off as well!

Figure 9.5　*C32 Class 2–4–2T at Southend in 1915*　　　LCGB K. Nunn Coll.

The Germans took the ship and the prisoners back to Zeebrugge, a Belgian port they controlled. Apparently they enjoyed an elaborate meal on the way, but the English stewardesses pretended not to have any wine on board.

Brussels stayed at Zeebrugge for five hours and was then taken to Bruges. The crew of 40 men and five stewardesses were locked up together in a cell at Bruges town hall; they were given only black bread and maggotty soup to eat.

The stewardesses were then put in a cattle train and taken to Ghent, where they spent another night in a slimy cellar. They were taken on to Cologne and eventually to a camp at Holzminden, from where they were returned to the border of neutral Holland.

The men were less fortunate. They were taken from Bruges to Ruhleben, from where they were scattered to several camps. Fryatt and First Officer Hartnell, however, were taken back from Ruhleben to Bruges where they were both questioned. The Germans had plans for Fryatt. On 27 July a Naval Court was set up, presided over by Commander von Yorke. Fryatt was charged with having attacked the U33 whilst being a non-combatant; his inscribed watches and English press cuttings were used as evidence against him. Mysteriously, the Captain of the U33 failed to appear as a witness.

Fryatt was found guilty and sentenced to death. Hartnell was told that it was to be Fryatt's last night and that he should stay with him, but at 6.30 pm it was announced that Fryatt was to be shot that evening.

At 7 pm Fryatt was taken out and shot, receiving 16 bullet wounds. He was buried in Bruges cemetery beneath a black cross. The German authorities posted a notice to explain the execution:

NOTICE – The English Captain of the Mercantile Marine, Charles Fryatt, of Southampton, though he did not belong to the armed forces of the enemy, attempted on 28 March 1915, to destroy a German submarine by running it down. This is the reason why he has been condemned to death by judgment of this day of the War Council of the Marine Corps and has been executed. A

Figure 9.6   *GER stewardesses from the* Brussels *at Holzminden camp in 1916*
Cambridgeshire Libraries

perverse action has thus received its punishment, tardy but just. Signed VON SCHRODER, Admiral Commandant of the Corps de Marine, Bruges, 27 July, 1916.

When rumours of Fryatt's execution reached England, there was a storm of outrage. The Imperial Merchant Service Guild called it 'the most despicable crime yet perpetrated by Germany'. The rumours were confirmed by Asquith in July when he stated, 'I deeply regret to say that it appears to be true that Captain Fryatt has been murdered by the Germans.' The story had been checked through the independent channel of the USA's ambassador to Belgium.

Lord Claud Hamilton of the GER observed, 'The latest act of the Hun is nothing less than sheer, brutal murder.' The GER awarded Fryatt's widow (who had seven children) a life pension of £25 per year, to which the Government added a further £100.

The Mayor of Harwich opened a memorial fund and a Fryatt memorial was put up in the booking hall at Liverpool Street in 1917, where it can be seen today. Fryatt's body was exhumed in 1919 and brought back to Britain for a service at St Paul's Cathedral. A special train then took the body to Dovercourt for burial, where his tomb can be seen in the churchyard.

Brussels itself was sunk off the Zeebrugge Mole in October 1918 during the famous British raid. It was salvaged in 1920 and sold off for use on Irish ferry services.

Of the other GER ships involved in the war, the *Clacton* was converted into a minesweeping auxiliary vessel and was torpedoed in the eastern Mediterranean on 3 August 1916. The *Colchester* was captured by the Germans whilst on the Tilbury to Rotterdam run in September 1916, and was later sunk. *Copenhagen* was torpedoed in the North Sea in March 1917 and *Newmarket* went down in similar fashion in 1918. *Dresden* was renamed *Louvain* in 1915 and was lost in the eastern Mediterranean on 21 January 1918; 224 men died.

The Great War was, of course, a catalyst for much social and economic change in Great Britain, and the railways did not escape. After the war had finished it was recognised that the railways were in need of great reorganisation, as a result of which the Great Eastern was absorbed into the London & North Eastern Railway group. A railway of unique character, but rather haphazard achievements, thus ceased to serve a region with which it had developed a special relationship.

Sources

Most of the material included in this book was found in company records formerly held by the British Transport Historical Archives and in the contemporary local press. Individual references have not always been given in these cases, but the nature of the information will normally indicate which type of source was used.

ACWORTH, W. M. (1889) *The Railways of England*. London.

BORLEY, H. V. (1982) *Chronology of London Railways*. Oakham.

CLINKER, C. R. (1978) *Clinker's Register of Closed Passenger Stations*. Bristol.

Eastern Counties Railway Minute Books, etc., in the Public Record Office, Kew.

Essex Record Office (1977) *Introduction to Ingatestone Hall*.

Essex Record Office (1978) *Railways in Essex*.

FOXWELL, E. and FARRER, T. C. (1889) *Express Trains, English and Foreign*. London.

GORDON, D. I. (1968) *A Regional History of the Railways of Great Britain*, Vol. V, *Eastern Counties*. Newton Abbot.

Great Eastern Railway Minute Books, etc.

HAINING, P. (1976) *The Great English Earthquake*. London.

Kelly's Directory of Essex, 1886, 1894.

Kelly's Directory of the Home Counties, 1845.

KETTON-CREMER, R. W. (1988) *Felbrigg*. London.

Maldon, Witham & Braintree Railway Minute Book and Subscription Lists.

MILES, H. D. (1906) *Pugilistica*. London.

PAYE, P. (1988) *The Mildenhall Branch*. Didcot.

Pigot & Co.'s Directory, 1839.

POND, C. C. (1982) *The Walthamstow and Chingford Railway*. Walthamstow.

RONEY, Cusack P. (1868) *Rambles on Railways*. London.

SIMMONS, J. (1986) *The Railway in Town and Country*. Newton Abbot.

White's History & Directory of Essex, 1848.

WILDE, E. (1913) *Ingatestone and the Great Essex Road*. Oxford.

Newspapers and Magazines

Braintree & Bocking Advertiser

Cambridge Chronicle

Essex Review

Essex Standard

Great Eastern Railway Magazine

Journal of the Railway and Canal Historical Society

The Locomotive Magazine

Norwich Mercury

Railway Magazine

Index